Ophiolatreia

Ophiolatreia

An account of the rites and mysteries connected with the origin, rise and development of serpent worship in various parts of the world, enriched with interesting traditions, and a full description of the celebrated serpent mounds & temples, the whole forming an exposition of one of the phases of phallic, or sex worship.

An Anonymous Scholar

OPHIOLATREIA
CHAPTER I

Ophiolatreia, the worship of the serpent, next to the adoration of the phallus, is one of the most remarkable, and, at first sight, unaccountable forms of religion the world has ever known. Until the true source from whence it sprang can be reached and understood, its nature will remain as mysterious as its universality, for what man could see in an object so repulsive and forbidding in its habits as this reptile, to render worship to, is one of the most difficult of problems to find a solution to. There is hardly a country of the ancient world, however, where it cannot be traced, pervading every known system of mythology, and leaving proofs of its existence and extent in the shape of monuments, temples, and earthworks of the most elaborate and curious character. Babylon, Persia, Hindostan, Ceylon, China, Japan, Burmah, Java, Arabia, Syria, Asia Minor, Egypt, Ethiopia, Greece, Italy, Northern and Western Europe, Mexico, Peru, America---all yield abundant testimony to the same effect, and point to the common origin of Pagan systems wherever found. Whether the worship was the result of fear or respect is a question that naturally enough presents itself, and in seeking to answer it we shall be confronted with the fact that in some places, as Egypt, the symbol was that of a good demon, while in India, Scandinavia, and Mexico, it was that of an evil one. It has been remarked that in the warmer regions of the globe, where this creature is the most formidable enemy which man can encounter, the serpent should be considered the mythological attendant of an evil being is not surprising, but that in the frozen or temperate regions of the earth, where he dwindles into the insignificances of a reptile without power to create alarm, he should be regarded in the same appalling character, is a fact which cannot be accounted for by natural causes. Uniformity of tradition can alone satisfactorily explain uniformity of superstition, where local circumstances are so discordant.

"The serpent is the symbol which most generally enters into the mythology of the world. It may in different countries admit among its fellow-satellites of Satan the most venomous or the most terrible of the animals in each country, but it preserves its own constancy, as the only invariable object of superstitious terror throughout the habitable world. 'Wherever the Devil reigned,' remarks Stillingfleet, 'the serpent was held in some peculiar veneration.' The universality of this singular and irrational, yet natural, superstition it is now proposed to show. Irrational, for there is nothing in common between deity and a reptile, to suggest the notion of Serpent-worship; and natural, because, allowing the truth of the events in Paradise, every probability is in favour of such a superstition springing up." (Deane.)

It may seem extraordinary that the worship of the serpent should ever have been introduced into the world, and it must appear still more remarkable that it should almost universally have prevailed. As mankind are said to have been ruined through the influence of this being, we could little expect that it would, of all other objects, have been adopted as the most sacred and salutary symbol, and rendered the chief object of adoration. Yet so we find it to have been, for in most of the ancient rites there is some allusion to it. In the orgies of Bacchus, the persons who took part in the ceremonies used to carry serpents in their hands, and with horrid screams call upon "Eva, Eva." They were often crowned with serpents while still making the same frantic exclamation. One part of the mysterious rites of Jupiter Sabazius was to let a snake slip down the bosom of the person to be initiated, which was taken out below. These ceremonies, and this symbolic worship, are said to have begun among the Magi, who were the sons of Chus, and by them they were propagated in various parts. Epiphanius thinks that the invocation "Eva, Eva," related to the great mother of mankind, who was deceived by the serpent, and Clemens of Alexandria is of the same opinion.

Others, however, think that Eva was the same as Eph, Epha, Opha, which the Greeks rendered Ophis, and by it denoted a serpent. Clemens acknowledges that the term Eva, properly aspirated, had such a signification.

Olympias, the mother of Alexander, was very fond of these orgies, in which the serpent was introduced. Plutarch mentions that rites of this sort were practised by the Edonian women near Mount Hæmus in Thrace, and carried on to a degree of madness. Olympias copied them closely in all their frantic manœuvres. She used to be followed with many attendants, who had each a thyrsus with serpents twined about it. They had also snakes in their hair, and in the chaplets which they wore, so that they made a most fearful appearance. Their cries also were very shocking, and the whole was attended with a continual repetition of the words, Evoe, Saboe, Hues Attes, Attes Hues, which were titles of the god Dionusus. He was peculiarly named Hues, and his priests were the Hyades and Hyautes. He was likewise styled Evas.

In Egypt was a serpent named Thermuthis, which was looked upon as very sacred; and the natives are said to have made use of it as a royal tiara, with which they ornamented the statues of Isis. We learn from Diodorus Siculus that the kings of Egypt wore high bonnets, which terminated in a round ball, and the whole was surrounded with figures of asps. The priests, likewise, upon their bonnets had the representation of serpents. The ancients had a notion that when Saturn devoured his own children, his wife Ops deceived him by substituting a large stone in lieu of one of his sons, which stone was called Abadir. But Ops and Opis, represented here as a feminine, was the serpent deity, and Abadir is the same personage under a different denomination. Abadir seems to be a variation of Ob-Adur, and signifies the serpent god Orus. One of these stones, which Saturn was supposed to have swallowed instead of a child, stood, according to Pausanias, at Delphi. It was esteemed very sacred, and used to have libations of wine poured upon it daily; and upon festivals was otherwise honoured. The purport of the above was probably this: it was for a long time a custom to offer children at the altar of Saturn; but in process of time they removed it, and in its room erected a stone pillar, before which they made their vows, and offered sacrifices of another nature. This stone which they thus substituted was called Ab-Adar, from the deity represented by it. The term Ab generally signifies a father, but in this instance it certainly relates to a serpent, which was indifferently styled Ab, Aub, and Ob. Some regard Abadon, or, as it is mentioned in the Book of Revelation, Abaddon, to have been the nameof the same Ophite god, with whose worship the world had been so long infected. He is termed Abaddon, the angel of the bottomless pit---the prince of darkness. In another place he is described as the dragon, that old serpent, which is the devil, and Satan. Hence the learned Heinsius is supposed to be right in the opinion which he has given upon this passage, when he makes Abaddon the same as the serpent Pytho.

It is said that in the ritual of Zoroaster the great expanse of the heavens, and even nature itself, was described under the symbol of a serpent. (Eusebius) The like was mentioned in the Octateuch of Ostanes; and moreover, in Peria and in other parts of the East they erected temples to the serpent tribe, and held festivals to their honour, esteeming them the supreme of all Gods, and the superintendents of the whole world. The worship began among the people of Chaldea. They built the city Opis upon the Tigris, and were greatly addicted to divination and to the worship of the serpent. From Chaldea the worship passed into Egypt, where the serpent deity was called Canoph, Caneph, and C'neph. It had also the name of Ob, or Oub, and was the same as the Basilicus, or Royal Serpent; the same also as the Thermuthis, and in like manner was made use of by way of ornament to the statues of their Gods. The chief Deity of Egypt is said to have been Vulcan, who was also styled Opas, as we learn from Cicero. He was the same as Osiris, the Sun; and hence was often called Ob-El, or Pytho Sol; and there were pillars sacred to him, with curious hieroglyphical inscriptions, which had the same name. They were very lofty, and narrow in comparison of their length; hence among the Greeks, who copied from the Egyptians, everything gradually tapering to a point was styled Obelos, and Obeliscus. Ophel (Oph-El) was a name of the same purport, and many sacred mounds, or Tapha, were thus denominated from the serpent Deity, to whom they were sacred.

Sanchoniathon makes mention of a history which he once wrote upon the worship of the serpent. The title of this work, according to Eusebius, was Ethothion, or Ethothia. Another treatise upon the same subject was written by Pherecydes Tyrus, which was probably a copy of the former; for he is said to have composed it from some previous accounts of the Phœnicians. The title of his book was the Theology of Ophion, styled Ophioneus, and his worshippers were called Ophionidæ. Thoth and Athoth were certainly titles of the Deity in the Gentile world; and the book of Sanchoniathon might very possibly have been from hence named Ethothion, or more truly, Athothion. But, from the subject upon which it was written, as well as from the treatise of Pherecydes, we have reason to think that Athothion, or Ethothion, was a mistake for Ath-Ophion, a title which more immediately related to that worship of which the writer treated. Ath was a sacred title, as we have shewn, and we imagine that this dissertation did not barely relate to the serpentine Deity, but contained accounts of his votaries, the Ophitæ, the principal of which were the sons of Chus. The worship of the serpent began among them, and they were from thence denominated Ethiopians, and Aithopians, which the Greeks render Aithiopes. They did not receive this name from their complexion, as has sometimes been surmised, for the branch of Phut and the Luhim, were probably of a deeper dye; but they were most likely so called from Ath-Ope, and Ath-Opis, the God which they worshipped. This may be shewn from Pliny. He says that the country Ethiopia (and consequently the people), had the name of Æthiop, from a personage who was a Deity---ab Æthiope Vulcani filio. The Æthiopes brought these rites into Greece, and called the island where they first established them Ellopia, Solis Serpentis, insula. It was the same as Eubœa, a name of the like purport, in which island was a region named Ethiopium. Eubœa is properly Oub-

Aia, and signifies the Serpent Island. The same worship prevailed among the Hyperboreans, as we may judge from the names of the sacred women who used to come annually to Delos; they were priestesses of the Tauric Goddess. Hercules was esteemed the chief God, the same as Chronus, and was said to have produced the Mundane egg. He was represented in the Orphic theology under the mixed symbol of a lion and a serpent, and sometimes of a serpent only.

The Cuthites, under the title of Heliadæ, having settled at Rhodes, as they were Hivites, or Ophites, the island was in consequence named Ophiusa. There was likewise a tradition that it had once swarmed with serpents. (Bochart says the island is said to have been named Rhodus from Rhad, a Syriac word for a serpent). The like notion prevailed almost in every place where they settled.

Fig. 2.—THE TEMPTATION, AS UNDERSTOOD IN THE EAST.

They came under the more general titles of Leleges and Pelasgi; but more particularly of Elopians, Europians, Oropians, Asopians, Inopians, Ophionians, and Æthiopes, as appears from the names which they bequeathed; and in most places where they resided there were handed down traditions which alluded to their original title of Ophites. In Phrygia, and upon the Hellespont, whither they sent out colonies very early, was a people styled the Ophiogeneis, or the serpent breed, who were said to retain an affinity and correspondence with serpents; and a notion prevailed that some hero, who had conducted them, was changed from a serpent to a man. In Colchis was a river Ophis, and there was another of the same name in Arcadia. It was so named from a body of people who settled upon its banks, and were said to have been conducted by a serpent.

It is said these reptiles are seldom found in islands, but that Tenos, one of the Cyclades, was supposed to have once swarmed with them. (Aristoph.)

Thucydides mentions a people of Ætotia, called Ophionians; and the temple of Apollo at Petara, in Lycia, seems to have had its first institution from a priestess of the same name. The island of Cyprus was called Ophiusa and Ophiodes, from the serpents with which it was supposed to have abounded. Of what species they were is nowhere mentioned, excepting only that about Paphos there was said to have been a kind of serpent with two legs. By this is meant the Ophite race, who came from Egypt, and from Syria, and got footing in this island. They settled also in Crete, where they increased greatly in numbers; so that Minos was said by an unseemly allegory, opheis ouresai, serpentes, minxisse. The island Seriphus was one vast rock, by the Romans called saxum scriphium, and made use of as a large kind of prison for banished persons. It is represented as having once abounded with serpents, and it is styled by Virgil, serpentifera, as the passage is corrected by Scaliger.

It is said by the Greeks that Medusa's head was brought by Perseus; by this is meant the serpent Deity, whose worship was here introduced by people called Peresians. Medusa's head denoted divine wisdom, and the island was sacred to the serpent, as is apparent from its name. The Athenians were esteemed Serpentiginæ, and they had a tradition that the chief guardian of their Acropolis was a serpent.

It is reported of the goddess Ceres that she placed a dragon for a guardian to her temple at Eleusis, and appointed another to attend upon Erectheus. Ægeus of Athens, according to Androtion, was of the serpent breed, and the first king of the country is said to have been a dragon. Others make Cecrops the first who reigned. He is said to have been of a two fold nature, being formed with the body of a man blended with that of a serpent. Diodorus says that this was a circumstance deemed by the Athenians inexplicable; yet he labours to explain it by representing Cecrops as half a man and half a brute, because he had been of two different communities. Eustathius likewise tries to solve it nearly upon the same principles, and with the like success. Some have said of Cecrops that he underwent a metamorphosis, being changed from a serpent to a man. By this was meant, according to Eustathius, that Cecrops by coming into Hellas divested himself of all the rudeness and barbarity of his country, and became more civilised and human. This is declared by some to be too high a compliment to be paid to Greece in its infant state, and detracts greatly from the character of the Egyptians. The learned Marsham therefore animadverts with great justice, "it is more probable that he introduced into Greece the urbanity of his own country, than that he was beholden to Greece for anything from thence." In respect to the mixed character of this personage, we may easily account for it. Cecrops was certainly a title of the Deity, who was worshipped under this emblam. Something of the like nature was mentioned of Triptolemus and Ericthonius, and the like has been said of Hercules. The natives of Thebes in Bœotia, like the Athenians, esteemed themselves of the serpent race. The Lacedæmonians likewise referred themselves to the same original. Their city is said of old to have swarmed with serpents. The same is said of the city Amyelæ in Italy, which was of Spartan origin. They came hither in such abundance that it was abandoned by the inhabitants. Argos was infested in the same manner till Apis came from Egypt and settled in that city. He was a prophet, the reputed son of Apollo, and a person of great skill and sagacity, and to him they attributed the blessing of having their country freed from this evil. Thus the Argives gave the credit to this imaginary personage of clearing their land of this grievance, but the brood came from the very quarter from whence Apis was supposed to have arrived. They were certainly Hivites from Egypt, and the same story is told of that country. It is represented as having been of old over-run with serpents, and almost depopulated through their numbers. Diodorus Siculus seems to understand this literally, but a region that was annually overflowed, and that too for so long a season, could not well be liable to such a calamity. They were serpents of another nature with which it was thus infested, and the history relates to the Cuthites, the original Ophitæ, who for a long time possessed that country. They passed from Egypt to Syria, and to the Euphrates, and mention is made of a particular breed of serpents upon that river, which were harmless to the natives but fatal to anybody else. This can hardly be taken literally; for whatever may be the wisdom of the serpent it cannot be sufficient to make these distinctions. These serpents were of the same nature as the birds of Diomedes, and the dogs in the temple of Vulcan; and the histories relate to Ophite priests, who used to spare their own people and sacrifice strangers, a custom which prevailed at one time in most parts of the world. The Cuthite priests are said to have been very learned; and, as they were Ophites, whoever had the advantage of their information was said to have been instructed by serpents.

As the worship of the serpent was of old so prevalent, many places, as well as people, from thence received their names. Those who settled in Campania were called Opici, which some would have changed to Ophici, because they were denominated from serpents. They are in reality both names of the same purport, and denote the origin of the people.

We meet with places called Opis, Ophis, Ophitæa, Ophionia, Ophioessa, Ophiodes, and Ophiusa. This last was an ancient name by which, according to Stephanus, the islands Rhodes, Cynthus, Besbicus, Tenos, and the whole continent of Africa, were distinguished. There were also cities so called. Add to these places denominated Oboth, Obona, and reversed, Onoba, from Ob, which was of the same purport.

Clemens Alexandrinus says that the term Eva signified a serpent if pronounced with a proper aspirate, and Epiphanius says the same thing. We find that there were places of this name.

There was a city Eva in Arcadia, and another in Macedonia. There was also a mountain Eva, or Evan, taken notice of by Pausanias, between which and Ithome lay the city Messene. He mentions also an Eva in Argolis, and speaks of it as a large town. Another name for a serpent, which we have not yet noticed, was Patan, or Pitan. Many places in different parts were denominated from this term. Among others was a city in Laconia, and another in Mysia, which Stephanus styles a city of Æolia. They were undoubtedly so named from the worship of the serpent, Pitan, and had probably Dracontia, which were figures and devices relative to the religion which prevailed. Ovid mentions the latter city, and has some allusions to its ancient history when he describes Medea as flying through the air from Athea to Colchis. The city was situate upon the ruin Eva, or Evan, which the Greeks rendered Evenus. According to Strabo it is compounded of Eva-Ain, the fountain or river of Eva the serpent.

It is remarkable that the Opici, who are said to have been named from serpents, had also the name of Pitanatæ; at least, one part of that family was so called. Pitanatæ is a term of the same purport as Opici, and relates to the votaries of Pitan, the serpent Deity, which was adored by that people. Menelaus was of old called Pitanates, as we learn from Hesychius, and the reason of it may be known from his being a Spartan, by which he was intimated one of the Serpentigenæ, or Ophites. Hence he was represented with a serpent for a device upon his shield. It is said that a brigade, or portion of infantry, was among some of the Greeks named Pitanates, and the soldiers in consequence of it must have been termed Pitanatæ, undoubtedly, because they had the Pitan, or serpent, for their standard. Analogous to this, among other nations there were soldiers called Draconarii. In most countries the military standard was an emblem of the Deity there worshipped.

What has already been said has thrown some light upon the history of this primitive idolatry, and we have shewn that wherever any of these Ophite colonies settled, they left behind from their rites and institutions, as well as from the names which they bequeathed to places, ample memorials, by which they may be clearly traced out.

CHAPTER II

Some persons are disposed to attribute to the Serpent, as a religious emblem, an origin decidedly phallic. Mr. C. S. Wake takes a contrary view, and says:---"So far as I can make out the serpent symbol has not a direct Phallic reference, nor is its attribute of wisdom the most essential. The idea most intimately associated with this animal was that of life, not present merely, but continued, and probably everlasting. Thus the snake Bai was figured as Guardian of the doorways of the Egyptian Tombs which represented the mansions of heaven. A sacred serpent would seem to have been kept in all the Egyptian temples, and we are told that many of the subjects, in the tombs of the kings at Thebes in particular, show the importance it was thought to enjoy in a future state. Crowns, formed of the Asp or sacred Thermuthis, were given to sovereigns and divinities, particularly to Isis, and these no doubt were intended to symbolise eternal life. Isis was a goddess of life and healing and the serpent evidently belonged to her in that character, seeing that it was the symbol also of other deities with the like attributes. Thus, on papyri it encircles the figure of Harpocrates, who was identified with Æsculapius; while not only was a great serpent kept alive in the great temple of Serapis, but on later monuments this god is represented by a great serpent with or without a human head. Mr. Fergusson, in accordance with his peculiar theory as to the origin of serpent worship, thinks this superstition characterised the old Turanaian (or rather let us say Akkadian) empire of Chaldea, while tree-worship was more a characteristic of the later Assyrian Empire. This opinion is no doubt correct, and it means really that the older race had that form of faith with which the serpent was always indirectly connected---adoration of the male principle of generation, the principal phase of which was probably ancestor worship, while the latter race adored the female principle, symbolised by the sacred tree, the Assyrian 'grove.' The 'tree of life,' however, undoubtedly had reference to the male element, and we may well imagine that originally the fruit alone was treated as symbolical of the opposite element."

Mr. J. H. Rivett-Carnac, in his paper printed in the journal of the Asiatic Society of Bengal, entitled "The Snake Symbol in India," suggests that the serpent is a symbol of the phallus. He says:---"The serpent appears on the prehistoric cromlechs and menhirs of Europe, on which I believe the remains of phallic worship may be traced. What little attention I have been able to give to the serpent symbol has been chiefly in its connection with the worship of Mahádeo or Siva, with a view to ascertain whether the worship of the snake and that of Mahádeo or the phallus may be considered identical, and whether the presence of the serpent on the prehistoric remains of Europe can be shown to support my theory, that the markings on the cromlechs and menhirs are indeed the traces of this form of worship, carried to Europe from the East by the tribes whose remains are buried beneath the tumuli.

During my visits to Benares, the chief centre of Siva worship in India, I have always carefully searched for the snake-symbol. On the most ordinary class of "Mahádeo," a rough stone placed on end supposed to represent the phallus, the serpent is not generally seen. But in the temples and in the better class of shrines which abound in the city and neighbourhood the snake is generally found encircling the phallus. The tail of the snakes is sometimes carried down the Yoni, and in one case I found two snakes on a shrine thus depicted.

In the Benares bazaar I once came across a splendid metal cobra, the head erect and hood expanded, so made as to be placed around or above a stone or metal "Mahádeo." It is now in England. The attitude of the cobra when excited and the expansion of the head will suggest the reason for this snake representing Mahádeo and the phallus.

Although the presence of the snake in these models cannot be said to prove much, and although from the easy adaptability of its form the snake must always have been a favourite subject in ornament, still it will be seen that the serpent is prominent in connection with the conventional shape under which Mahádeo is worshipped at Benares and elsewhere, that it sometimes takes the place of the Linga, and that it is to be found entwined with almost every article connected with this worship."

Further on the same writer says:---"The Nág panchami or fifth day of the moon in Sawan is a great fete in the city of Nágpúr, and more than usual license is indulged in on that day. Rough pictures of snakes in all sorts of shapes and positions are sold and distributed, something after the manner of valentines. I cannot find any copies of these queer sketches, and if I could they would hardly be fit to be reproduced. Mr. J. W. Neill, the present Commissioner of Nágpúr, was good enough to send me some superior valentines of this class, and I submit them now for the inspection of the Society. It will be seen that in these paintings, some of which are not without merit either as to design or execution, no human figures are introduced. In the ones I have seen in days gone by the positions of the women with the snakes were of the most indecent description and left no doubt that, so far as the idea represented in these sketches was concerned, the cobra was regarded as the phallus. In the pictures now sent the snakes will be seen represented in congress in the well-known form of the Caduceus Esculapian rod. Then the many-headed snake, drinking from the jewelled cup, takes me back to some of the symbols of the mysteries of bygone days. The snake twisted round the tree and the second snake approaching it are suggestive of the temptation and fall. But I am not unmindful of the pitfalls from which Wilford suffered, and I quite see that it is not impossible that this picture may be held to be not strictly Hindu in its treatment. Still the tree and the serpent are on the brass models which accompany this paper, and which I have already shewn are to be purchased in the Benares Brass Bazaar of to-day---many hundreds of miles away from Nágpúr where these Valentines were drawn.

In my paper on the Kumáon Rock Markings, besides noting the resemblance between the cup markings of India and Europe, I hazarded the theory that the concentric circles and certain curious markings of what some have called the 'jew's harp' type, so common in Europe, are traces of Phallic worship carried there by tribes whose hosts descended into India, pushed forward into the remotest corners of Europe, and, as their traces seem to suggest, found their way on to the American Continent too. Whether the markings really ever were intended to represent the Phallus and the Yoni must always remain a matter of opinion. But I have no reason to be dissatisfied with the reception with which this, to many somewhat pleasant theory, has met in some of the Antiquarian Societies of Europe.

No one who compares the stone Yonis of Benares, sent herewith, with the engravings on the first page of the work on the Rock Markings of Northumberland and Argyleshire, published privately by the Duke of Northumberland, will deny that there is an extraordinary resemblance between the conventional symbol of Siva worship of to-day and the ancient markings on the rocks, menhirs, and cromlechs of Northumberland, of Scotland, of Brittany, of Scandinavia, and other parts of Europe.

And a further examination of the forms of the cromlechs and tumuli and menhirs will suggest that the tumuli themselves were intended to indicate the symbols of the Mahádeo and Yoni, conceived in no obscene sense, but as representing regeneration, the new life, "life out of death, life everlasting," which those buried in the tumuli, facing towards the sun in its meridian, were expected to enjoy in the hereafter. Professor Stephens, the well-known Scandinavian Antiquary, writing to me recently, speaks of the symbols as follows:---"The pieces (papers) you were so good as to send me were very valuable and welcome. There can be no doubt that it is to India we have to look for the solution of many of our difficult archæological questions."

"But especially interesting is your paper on the Ancient Rock-Sculpturings. I believe that you are quite right in your views. Nay, I go further. I think that the northern Bulb-stones are explained by the same combination. I therefore send you the Swedish Archæological Journal for 1876, containing Baron Herculius' excellent dissertation on these objects......You can examine the many excellent woodcuts. I look upon these things as late conventionalized abridgments of the Linga and Yoni, life out of death, life everlasting---thus a fitting ornament for the graves of the departed."

The author further says:---"Many who indignantly repudiate the idea of the prevalence of Phallic Worship among our remote ancestors hold that these symbols represent the snake or the sun. But admitting this, may not the snake, after all, have been but a symbol of the phallus? And the sun, the invigorating power of nature, has ever, I believe, been considered to represent the same idea, not necessarily obscene, but the great mystery of nature, the life transmitted from generation to generation, or, as Professor Stephans puts it, 'life out of death, life everlasting.'" The same idea, in fact, which, apart from any obscene conception, causes the rude Mahádeo and Yoni to be worshipped daily by hundreds of thousands of Hindus.

Brown, in his "Great Dionysiak Myth," says:---"The Serpent has six principal points of connection with Dionysos: 1---As a symbol of, and connected with, wisdom. 2---As a solar emblem. 3---As a symbol of time and eternity. 4---As an emblem of the earth, life. 5---As connected with fertilizing moisture. 6---As a phallic emblem."

Referring to the last of these, he proceeds---"The serpent being connected with the sun, the earth life and fertility must needs be also a phallic emblem, and so appropriate to the cult of Dionysos Priapos. Mr. Cox after a review of the subject, observes, 'Finally, the symbol of the Phallus suggested the form of the serpent, which thus became the emblem of life and healing. There then we have the key to that tree and serpent worship which has given rise to much ingenious speculation.' The myth of the serpent and the tree is not, I apprehend, exhausted by any merely phallic explanation, but the phallic element is certainly one of the most prominent features in it, as it might be thought any inspection of the carvings connected with the Topes of Sanchi and Amravati would show. It is hard to believe, with Mr. Fergusson, that the usefulness and beauty of trees gained them the payment of divine honours. Again, the Asherah or Grove-cult (Exod. 34, 13; I Kings 17, 16; Jer. 17, 2; Micah 5, 14) was essentially Phallic, Asherah being the Upright. It seems also to have been in some degree connected with that famous relic, the brazen serpent of Nehushtan (2 Kings 18, 4). Donaldson considers that the Serpent is the emblem of desire. It has also been suggested that the creature symbolised sensation generally."

The Sir G. W. Cox referred to above, in his "Mythology of Argai Nations," says:---"If there is one point more certain than another it is that wherever tree and serpent worship has been found, the cultus of the Phallos and the Ship, of the Linga and Yoni, in connection with the worship of the sun, has been found also. It is impossible to dispute the fact, and no explanation can be accepted for one part of the cultus which fails to explain the other. It is unnecessary, therefore, to analyze theories which profess to see in it the worship of the creeping brute or the wide-spreading tree. A religion based on the worship of the venomous reptile must have been a religion of terror; in the earliest glimpses which we have of it, the serpent is a symbol of life and of love. Nor is the Phallic cultus in any respect a cultus of the full-grown and branching tree. In its earliest form the symbol is everywhere a mere stauros, or pole; and although this stock or rod budded in the shape of the thyrsus and the shepherd's staff, yet, even in its latest developments, the worship is confined to small bushes and shrubs and diminutive plants of a particular kind. Nor is it possible again to dispute the fact that every nation, at some stage or other of its history, has attached to this cultus precisely that meaning which the Brahman now attaches to the Linga and the Yoni. That the Jews clung to it in this special sense with vehement tenacity is the bitter compaint of the prophets; and the crucified serpent adored for its healing powers stood untouched in the Temple until it was removed and destroyed by Hezekiah. This worship of serpents, "void of reason," condemned in the Wisdom of Solomon, probably survived even the Babylonish captivity. Certainly it was adopted by the Christians who were known as Ophites, Gnostics, and Nicolaitans. In Athenian mythology the serpent and the tree are singularly prominent. Kekrops, Erechtheus, and Erichthonios, are each and all serpentine in the lower portion of their bodies. The sacred snake of Athênê had its abode in the Akropolis, and her olive trees secured for her the victory in her rivalry with Poseidôn. The health-giving serpent lay at the feet of Asklêpios and snakes were fed in his temple at Epidauros and elsewhere. That the ideas of mere terror and death suggested by the venomous or the crushing reptile could never have given way thus completely before those of life, healing, and safety, is obvious enough; and the latter ideas alone are associated with the serpent as the object of adoration. The deadly beast always was, and has always remained, the object of horror and loathing which is expressed for Ahi, the choking and throttling snake, the Vritra whom Indra smites with his unerring lance, the dreadful Azidahaka of the Avesta, the Zohak or Biter of modern Persian mythology, the serpents whom Heraktes strangles in his cradle, the Python, or Fafnir, or Grendel, or Sphinx whom Phoibos, or Sigurd, or Beowulf, or Oidipous smite and slay. That the worship of the Serpent has nothing to do with these evil beasts is abundantly clear from all the Phallic monuments of the East or West. In the topes of Sanchi and Amravati the disks which represent the Yoni predominate in every part of the design; the emblem is worn with unmistakeable distinctness by every female figure, carved within these disks, while above the multitude are seen, on many of the disks, a group of women with their hands resting on the linga, which they uphold. It may, indeed, be possible to trace out the association which connects the Linga with the bull in Sivaison, as denoting more particularly the male power, while the serpent in Jainaison and Vishnavism is found with the female emblem, the Yoni. So again in Egypt, some may discern in the bull Apis or Mnevis the predominance of the male idea in that country, while in Assyria or Palestine the Serpent or Agathos Daimon is connected with the altar of Baal.

CHAPTER III

"By comparing all the vaired legends of the East and West in conjunction," says a learned author, "we obtain the following outline of the mythology of the Ancients: It recognises, as the primary elements of things, two independent principles of the nature of Male and Female; and these, in mystic union, as the soul and body, constitute the Great Hermaphrodite Deity, THE ONE, the universe itself, consisting still of the two separate elements of its composition, modified though combined in one individual, of which all things are regarded but as parts......If we investigate the Pantheons of the ancient nations, we shall find that each, notwithstanding the variety of names, acknowledged the same deities and the same system of theology; and, however humble any of the deities may appear, each who has any claim to antiquity will be found ultimately, if not immediately, resolvable into one or other of the Primeval Principles, the Great God and Goddess of the Gentiles." (Cory's Ancient Fragments, Intro. 34)

"We must not be surprised," says Sir William Jones, "at finding, on a close examination, that the characters of all the Pagan deities, male and female, melt into each other, and at last into one or two, for it seems a well-founded opinion that the whole crowd of gods and goddesses in ancient Rome and modern Váránes mean only the Powers of Nature, and principally those of the Sun, expressed in a variety of ways and by a multitude of fanciful names."

The doctrine of the Reciprocal Principles of Nature, designated as active and passive, male and female, and often symbolized as the Sun and Moon, or the Sun and the Earth, was distinctly recognised in the mythological systems of America. It will be well to notice the rationale of this doctrine, and some of the more striking forms which, in the development of human ideas, it has assumed; for it may safely be claimed that under some of its aspects or modifications it has entered into every religious system, if, indeed, it has not been the nucleus of every mythology.

The idea of a creation, suggested by the existence of things, was, no doubt, the first result of human reasoning. The mode of the event, the manner in which it was brought about, was, it is equally unquestionable, the inquiry which next occupied the mind, and man deduced from the operations of nature around him his first theory of creation. From the egg, after incubation, he saw emerging the living bird, a phenomenon which, to his simple apprehension, was nothing less than an actual creation. How naturally then, how almost of necessity, did that phenomenon, one of the most obvious in nature, associate itself with his ideas of creation---a creation which he could not help recognising, but which he could not explain. The extent to which the egg, received as a symbol, entered into the early cosmogonies will appear in another and more appropriate connection.

By a similar process did the creative power come to be symbolized under the form of the Phallus, in it was recognised the cause of reproduction, or, as it appeared to the primitive man, of creation. So the Egyptians, in their refinement upon this idea, adopted the scarabæus as a symbol of the First Cause, the great hermaphrodite Unity, for the reason that they believed that insect to be both male and female, capable of self-inception and singular production, and possessed of the power of vitalizing its own work.

It is well known that the Nymphœ, Lotus, or Water-Lily is held sacred throughout the East, and the various sects of that quarter of the globe represent their deities, either decorated with its flowers, holding it as a sceptre, or seated on a lotus throne or pedestal. "It is," says Maurice, "the sublime and hallowed symbol that perpetually occurs in oriental mytholgy, and not without substantial reason; for it is itself a lovely prodigy, and contains a treasure of physical instruction." The reason of its adoption as a symbol is explained by Mr. Payne Knight, and affords a beautiful illustration of the rationale of symbolism, and of the profound significance often hidden beneath apparently insignificant emblems. "This plant," observes Mr. Knight, "grows in the water, and amongst its broad leaves puts forth a flower, in the centre of which is formed its seed vessel, shaped like a bell or inverted cone, and punctured on the top with little cavities or cells, in which the seeds grow. The orifice of these cells being too small to let the seeds drop out when ripe, they shoot forth into new plants in the places where they are formed; the bulb of the vessel serving as a matrix to nourish them until large enough to burst it open and release themselves, after which, like other aquatic plants, they take root wherever the current deposits them. The plant, therefore, being thus productive of itself, and vegetating from its own matrix, without being fostered in the earth, was naturally adopted as a symbol of the productive power of waters upon which the active Spirit of the Creator acted in giving life and vegetation to matter. We accordingly find it employed in every part of the northern hemisphere where the symbolical religion, improperly called idolatry, existed."

Examples quoted illustrate the inductive powers by which unsided reason arrives at its results, as well as the means by which it indicates them in the absence of a written language or of one capable of conveying abstract ideas. The mythological symbols of all early nations furnish ample evidence that it was thus they embodied or shadowed forth their conceptions---the germ of a symbolic system, which was afterwards extended to every manifestation of nature and every attribute of Divinity.

We may in this manner rationally and satisfactorily account for the origin of the doctrine of the reciprocal principles. Its universal acceptance establishes that it was deduced from the operations of that law so obviously governing all animated nature---that of reproduction or procreation.

In the Egyptian mythology, the Divine Osiris was venerated as the active, dispensing, or originating energy, and was symbolized as the Sun; Iris as terrene nature, the passive recipient, the producer; their annual offspring was Horus, the vernal season or infant year. The poet Hesiod, in the beginning of his Theogony, distinguishes the male and female, or generative and productive powers of Nature, as Ouranus and Gaia, Heaven and

Earth. The celestial emblems of these powers were usually, as we have said, the Sun and Moon; the terrestrial, Fire and Earth. They were designed as Father and Mother; and their more obvious symbols, as has already been intimated, were the Phallus and Kteis, or the Lingam and Yoni of Hindustan.

That the worship of the phallus passed from India or from Ethiopia into Egypt, from Egypt into Asia Minor, and into Greece, is not so much a matter of astonishment---these nations communicated with each other; but that this worship existed in countries a long time unknown to the rest of the world---in many parts of America, with which the people of the Eastern Continent had formerly no communication---is an astonishing but well attested fact. When Mexico was discovered, there was found in the city of Panuco, the particular worship of the Phallus well established, its image was adorned in the temples; there were in the public places bas reliefs, which like those of India, represented in various manners the union of the two sexes. At Tlascalla, another city of Mexico, they revered the act of generation under the united symbols of the characteristic organs of the two sexes. Garcilasso de la Vega says---"that according to Blas Valera, the God of Luxury was called Tiazolteuli," but some writers say, "this is a mistake." One of the goddesses of the Mexican Pantheon was named Tiazolteotl, which Boturini describes as Venus unchaste, low, and abominable, the hieroglyphic of these men and women who are wholly abandoned, mingling promiscuously one with another, gratifying their bestial appetites like animals. Boturini is said to be not entirely correct in his apprehensions of the character of this goddess. She is Cinteotl, the goddess of Maize, under another aspect. Certain of the temples of India abound with sculptured representations of the symbols of Phallic Worship, and if we turn to the temples of Central America, which in many respects exhibit a strict correspondence with those of India, we find precisely the same symbols, separate and in combination.

CHAPTER IV

The ancient monuments of the Western United States consist for the most part of elevations and embankments of earth and stone, erected with great labour and manifest design. In connection with these, more or less intimate, are found various minor relics of art, consisting of ornaments and implements of many kinds, some of them composed of metal but most of stone.

These remains are spread over a vast amount of country. They are found on the sources of the Alleghany, in the western part of the state of New York on the east; and extend thence westwardly along the southern shore of Lake Erie, and through Michigan and Wisconsin, to Iowa and the Nebraska territory on the west. Some ancient works, probably belonging to the same system with those of the Mississippi valley and erected by the same people, occur upon the Susquehanna river as far down as the Valley of Wyoming in Pennsylvania. The mound builders seem to have skirted the southern border of Lake Erie, and spread themselves in diminished numbers over the western part of the State of New York, along the shores of Lake Ontario to the St. Lawrence river. They penetrated into the interior, eastward, as far as the county of Onondaga, where some slight vestiges of their work still exist. These seem to have been their limits at the northeast. We have no record of their occurrence above the great lakes. Carner mentions some on the shores of Lake Pepin, and some are said to occur near Lake Travers, under the 46th parallel of latitude. Lewis and Clark saw them on the Missouri river, one thousand miles above its junction with the Mississippi; and they have been observed on the Kanzas and Platte and on other remote western rivers. They are found all over the intermediate country, and spread over the valley of the Mississippi to the Gulf of Mexico. They line the shores of the Gulf from Texas to Florida, and extend in diminished numbers into South Carolina. They occur in great numbers in Ohio, Indiana, Illinois, Wisconsin, Missouri,

Arkansas, Kentucky, Tennessee, Louisiana, Mississippi, Alabama, Georgia, Florida and Texas. They are found in less numbers in the Western portions of New York, Pennsylvania, Virginia, and North and South Carolina; as also in Michigan, Iowa, and in the Mexican territory beyond the Rio Grande del Norte. In short, they occupy the entire basin of the Mississippi and its tributaries, as also the fertile plains along the Gulf.

Although possessing throughout certain general points of resemblance going to establish a kindred origin, these works, nevertheless, resolve themselves into three grand geographical divisions, which present in many respects striking contrasts, yet so gradually merge into each other that it is impossible to determine where one series terminates and the other begins. In the region bordering upon the upper lakes, to a certain extent in Michigan, Iowa and Missouri, but particularly in Wisconsin, we find a succession of remains, entirely singular in their form and presenting but slight analogy to any others of which we have in any portion of the globe. The larger proportion of these are structures of earth bearing the forms of beasts, birds, reptiles, and even of men; they are frequently of gigantic dimensions, constituting huge basso-relievos upon the face of the country. They are very numerous and in most cases occur in long and apparently dependent ranges. In connection with them are found many conical mounds and occasional short lines of embankment, in rare instances forming enclosures. These animal effigies are mainly confined to Wisconsin, and extend across the territory from Ford du Lac in a south-western direction, ascending the Fox river and following the general course of Rock and Wisconsin rivers to the Mississippi. They may be much more extensively disseminated; but it is here only that they have been observed in considerable numbers. In Michigan, as also in Iowa and Missouri, similar elevations of more or less outline are said to occur. They are represented as dispersed in ranges like the buildings of a modern city, and covering sometimes an arc of many acres.

The number of these ancient remains is well calculated to excite surprise, and has been adduced in support of the hypothesis that they are most if not all of them natural formations, "the result of diluvial action," modified perhaps in some instances, but never erected by man. Of course no such suggestion was ever made by individuals who had enjoyed the opportunity of seeing and investigating them. Simple structures of earth could not possibly bear more palpable evidences of an artificial origin than do most of the western monuments. The evidences in support of this assertion, derived from the form, structure, position and contents of these remains, sufficiently appear in the pages of this work.

The structure, not less than the form and position of a large number of the Earthworks of the West, and especially of the Scioto valley, render it clear that they were erected for other than defensive purposes. The small dimensions of most of the circles, the occurrence of the ditch interior to the embankments, and the fact that many of them are comletely commanded by adjacent heights, are some of the circumstances which may be mentioned as sustaining this conclusion. We must seek, therefore, in the connection in which these works are found and in the character of the mounds, if such there be within their walls, for the secret of their origin. And it may be observed that it is here we discover evidences still more satisfactory and conclusive than are furnished by their small dimensions and other circumstances above mentioned, that they were not intended for defence. Thus, when we find an enclosure containing a number of mounds, all of which it is capable of demonstration were religious in their purposes or in some way connected with the superstitions of the people who built them, the conclusion is irresistible that the enclosure itself was also deemed sacred and thus set apart as "tabooed" or consecrated ground---especially when it is obvious at the first glance that it possesses none of the requisites of a military work. But it is not to be concluded that those enclosures alone, which contain mounds of the description here named, were designed for sacred purposes. We have reason to believe that the religious system of the mound builders, like that of the Aztecs, exercised among them a great if not controlling influence. Their government may have been, for aught we know, a government of priesthood; one in which the priestly and civil functions were jointly exercised, and one sufficiently powerful to have secured in the Mississippi valley, as it did in Mexico, the erection of many of those vast monuments which for ages will continue to challenge the wonder of men. There may have been certain superstitious ceremonies, having no connection with the purposes of the mounds, carried on in the enclosures specially dedicated to them. It is a conclusion which every day's investigation and observation has tended to confirm, that most, perhaps all, of the earthworks not manifestly defensive in their character were in some way connected with the superstitious rights of the builders, though in what manner, it is, and perhaps ever will be, impossible satisfactorily to determine.

By far the most extraordinary and interesting earthwork discovered in the West is the great Serpent, situate on Brush Creek at a point known as the "Three Forks," near the north line of Adams county, Ohio. It occupies the summit of a high crescent-form hill or spur of land, rising a hundred and fifty feet above the level of Brush Creek, which washes its base. The side of the hill next the stream presents a perpendicular wall of rock, while the other slopes rapidly, though it is not so steep as to preclude cultivation. The top of the hill is not level but slightly convex, and presents a very even surface one hundred and fifty feet wide by one thousand long, measuring from its extremity to the point where it connects with the table land. Conforming to the curve of the hill and occupying its very summit is the serpent, its head resting near the point and its body winding back for seven hundred feet in graceful undulations, terminating in a triple coil at the tail. The entire length, if extended, would be not less than one thousand feet. The neck of the serpent is stretched out and slightly curved, and its mouth is opened wide as if in the act of swallowing or ejecting an oval figure which rests partially within the distended jaws. This oval is formed by an embankment of earth, without any perceptible opening, four feet in height, and is perfectly regular in outline, its transverse and conjugate diameters being one hundred and sixty and eighty feet respectively. The ground within the oval is slightly elevated; a small circular elevation of large stones much burned once existed in its centre, but they have been thrown down and scattered by some ignorant visitor, under the prevailing impression probably that gold was hidden beneath them. The point of the hill within which this egg-shaped figure rests seems to have been artificially cut to conform to its outline, leaving a smooth platform, ten feet wide and somewhat inclining inwards, all around it.

Upon either side of the serpent's head extend two small triangular elevations ten or twelve feet over. They are not high, and although too distinct to be overlooked, are yet much too much obliterated to be satisfactorily traced.

An effigy in the form of an alligator occurs near Granville, Licking county, Ohio, upon a high hill or headland; in connection with which there are unmistakeable evidences of an altar, similar to that in conjunction with the work just named. It is known in the vicinity as "the Alligator," which designation has been adopted for want of a better, although the figure bears as close a resemblance to the lizard as any other reptile. It is placed transversely to the point of land on which it occurs, the head pointing to the south-west. The total length from the point of the nose following the curve of the tail to the tip is about two hundred and fifty feet, the breadth of the body forty feet, and the length of the feet or paws each thirty-six feet. The ends of the paws are a little broader than the remaining portions of the same, as if the spread of the toes had been originally indicated. Some parts of the body are more elevated than others, an attempt having evidently been made to preserve the proportions of the object copied. The outline of the figure is clearly defined; its average height is not less than four feet; at the shoulders it is six feet in altitude. Upon the inner side of the effigy is an elevated circular space covered with stones which have been burned. This has been denominated an altar.

It seems more than probable that this singular effigy, like that last described, had its origin in the superstition of its makers.

It was perhaps the high place where sacrifices were made on stated or extraordinary occasions, and where the ancient people gathered to celebrate the rites of their unknown worship. Its position and all the circumstances attending it certainly favour such a conclusion.

The same is true of a work in the form of a cross, occupying a like situation near the village of Tarlton, Pickaway County, Ohio. From these premises, we are certainly justified in concluding that these several effigies had probably a cognate design, possessed a symbolical significance, and were conspicuous objects of religious regard, and that on certain occasions sacrifices were made on the altars within or near them.

The only structures sustaining any analogy to these are found in Wisconsin and the extreme North-West. There we find great numbers of mounds bearing the forms of animals of various kinds, and entering into a great variety of combinations with each other, and with conical mounds and lines of embankments, which are also abundant. They are usually found on the low, level, or undulating prairies, and seldom in such conspicuous positions as those discovered in Ohio. Whether they were built by the same people with the latter, and had a common design and purpose, it is not undertaken to say, nor is it a question into which we propose to enter.

It is an interesting fact that amongst the animal effigies of Wisconsin, structures in the form of serpents are of frequent occurrence.

Some years ago, Mr. Pigeon, of Virginia, made drawings of a number of these, and he stated that near the junction of the St. Peter's with the Mississippi River were a large number of mounds and monuments, consisting---1st, of a circle and square in combination, as at Circleville, in Ohio, the sole difference being a large truncated mound in the centre of the square, as well as in the centre of the circle, with a platform round its base; 2nd, near by, the effigy of a gigantic animal resembling the elk, in length one hundred and ninety-five feet; 3rd, in the same vicinity, a large conical mound, three hundred feet in diameter at the base, and thirty feet in height, its summit covered with charcoal. This mound was surrounded by one hundred and twenty smaller mounds, disposed in the form of a circle. Twelve miles to the westward of these, and within sight of them, was a large conical truncated mound, sixty feet in diameter at the bottom, and eighteen feet high, built upon a raised platform or bottom. It was surrounded by a circle three hundred and sixty five feet in circumference. Entwined around this circle, in a triple coil, was an embankment, in the form of a serpent, two thousand three hundred and ten feet in length. This embankment, at the centre of the body, was eighteen feet in diameter, but diminished towards the head and tail in just proportion. The elevation of the head was four feet, of the body six feet, of the tail two feet. The central mound was capped with blue clay, beneath which was sand mixed with charcoal and ashes.

Mounds arranged in serpentine form have also been found in Iowa, at a place formerly known as Prairie La Porte, afterwards called Gottenburgh. Also at a place seven miles north of these on Turkey River, where the range was two and a half miles long, the mounds occurring at regular intervals. Twenty miles to the westward of this locality was the effigy of a great serpent with that of a tortoise in front of its mouth. This structure was found to be one thousand and four feet long, eighteen feet broad at its widest part, and six feet high; the tortoise was eighteen by twelve feet.

Mr. Pigeon gave accounts of many other structures, tending to illustrate and confirm the opinions advanced respecting the religious and symbolical character and design of many, if not all, the more regular earth-works of the Western States. Thirty miles west of Prairie Du Chien, he found a circle enclosing a pentagon, which in its turn enclosed another circle, within which was a conical truncated mound. The outer circle was twelve hundred feet in circumference, the embankment twelve feet broad and from three to five feet high. The entrance was on the east. The mound was thirty-six feet in diameter by twelve feet high. Its summit was composed of white pipe-clay, beneath which was found a large quantity of mica in sheets. It exhibited abundant traces of fire.

Four miles distant from this, on the lowlands of the Kickapoo River, Mr. Pigeon discovered a mound with eight radiating points, undoubtedly designed to represent the Sun. It was sixty feet in diameter at the base, and three feet high. The points extended outwards about nine feet. Surrounding this mound were five crescent-shaped mounds so arranged as to constitute a circle. Many analogous structures were discovered at other places, both in Wisconsin and Iowa. At Cappile Bluffs, on the Mississippi River, were found a conical, truncated mound, surrounded by nine radiating effigies of men, the heads pointing inwards.

Probably no one will hesitate in ascribing the work just described, some extraordinary significance. It cannot be supposed to be the offspring of an idle fancy or a savage whim. It bears, in its position and the harmony of its structure, the evidences of design, and it seems to have been begun and finished in accordance with a matured plan, and not to have been the result of successive and unmeaning combinations. It is probably not a work for defence, for there is nothing to defend; on the contrary, it is clearly and unmistakably, in form and attitude, the representation of a serpent, with jaws distended, in the act of swallowing or ejecting an oval figure, which may be distinguished, from the suggestions of analogy, as an egg. Assuming for the entire structure a religious origin, it can be regarded only as the recognised symbol of some grand mythological idea. What abstract conception was thus embodied; or what vast even thus typically commemorated, we have no certain means of knowing! Analogy, however, although too often consulted on trivial grounds, furnishes us with gleams of light, of greater or less steadiness, as our appeals to its assistance happen to be conducted, on every subject connected with man's beliefs. We proceed now to discover what light reason and analogy shed upon the singular structure before us.

Naturally, and almost of necessity, the egg became associated with man's primitive idea of creation. It aptly symbolised that primordial, quiescent state of things which preceded their vitalization and activity---the inanimate chaos, before life began, when "the earth was without form and void, and darkness was upon the face of the deep." It was thus received in the early cosmogonies, in all of which the vivification of the Mundane Egg constituted the act of creation; from it sprang the world resplendent in glory and teeming with life.

Faber says---"The ancient pagans, in almost every part of the globe, were wont to symbolize the world by an Egg. Hence this symbol is introduced into the cosmogonies of nearly all nations, and there are few persons even among those who have not made mythology their study, to whom the Mundane Egg is not perfectly familiar. It was employed, not only to represent the earth but also the Universe in its largest extent." (Origin Pagan Idol., Vol. I, p. 175)

"The world," says Menu, "was all darkness, undiscernible, undistinguishable, altoghether in a profound sleep, till the Self-Existent, Invisible God (Brahm), making it manifest with five elemtents and other glorious forms, perfectly dispelled the gloom. Desiring to raise up creatures by an emanation from his own essence, he first created the waters, and inspired them with power of motion; by that power was produced a golden egg, blazing like a thousand stars, in which was born Brahma, the great parent of national beings, that which is the invisible cause, self-existent, but unperceived. This divinity having dwelt in the Egg through revolving years, himself meditating upon himself, divided into two equal parts, and from these halves he framed the heavens and the earth, placing in the midst the subtil ether, the eight points of the world, and the permanent receptacle of the waters."

The above is Maurice's translation. Sir William Jones renders it:---"The sole, self-existent power, having willed to produce various beings from his own divine substance, first, with a thought created the waters, and placed in them a productive seed. That seed became an egg, bright as gold, blazing like the luminary with a thousand beams, and in that egg ws born himself, in the form of Brahma, the great forefather of all spirits."

Aristophanes, in his Comedy of the Birds, is thought to have given the notions of cosmogony, ancient even in his days. "Chaos, Night, black Erebus, and wide Tartarus first existed: there was neither earth, nor air, nor heaven; but in the bosom of Erebus black-winged Night produced an Aerial Egg, from which was born golden-pinioned Love (Phanes), and he, the Great Universal Father, begot our race out of dark Chaos, in the midst of widespreading Tartarus, and called us into light."

We find this conception clearly embodied in one of the Orphic fragments, the Hymn to Protogones, who is equivalent to Phanes, the Life-giver, Priapus, or Generator.

"I invoke thee, oh Protogones, two-fold, great, wandering through the ether;

Egg-Born rejoicing in thy golden wings;

Bull-faced, the Generator of the blessed and of mortal men;

The much-renowned Light, the far celebrated Ericapæus;

Ineffiable, occult, impetuous all-glittering strength;

Who scatterest the twilight cloud of darkness from the eyes,

And roam'st through the world upon the flight of thy wings,

Bringing forth the brilliant and all-pure light; wherefore I invoke thee, as Phanes,

As Priapus the King, and as the dark-faced splendour,---

Come, thou blessed being, full of Metis (wisdom) and generation come in joy

To thy sacred, ever-varying mysteries."

We have, according to these early notions, the egg representing Being simply; Chaos, the great void from which, by the will of the superlative Unity, proceeds the generative or creative influence, designated among the Greeks as "Phanes," "Golden-pinioned Love," "The Universal Father," "Egg-born Protogones" (the latter Zeus or Jupiter); in India as "Brahma," the "Great Parent of Rational Creatures," the "Father of the Universe;" and in Egypt as "Ptha," the "Universal Creator."

The Chinese, whose religious conceptions correspond generally with those of India, entertained similar notions of the origin of things. They set forth that Chaos, before the creation, existed in the form of a vast egg, in which was contained the principles of all things. Its vivification, among them also, constituted the act of creation.

According to this and other authorities, the vivification of the Mundane Egg is allegorically represented in the temple of Daibod, in Japan, by a nest egg, which is shown floating in an expanse of waters against which a bulb (everywhere an emblem of generative energy, and prolific heat, the Sun) is striking with his horns.

"Near Lemisso, in the Island of Cyprus, is still to be seen a gigantic egg-shaped vase, which is supposed to represent the Mundane or Orphic Egg. It is of stone, and measures thrity feet in cirumference. Upon one side, in a semi-circlar niche, is sculptured a bull, the emblem of productive energy. This figure is understood to signify the Tauric constellation, "The Stars of Abundance," with the heliacal or cosmical rising of which was connected the return of the mystic reinvigorating principle of animal fecundity." (Landseer's Sabæan Res.)

In the opinion above mentioned, many other nations of the ancient world, the Egyptians, the Assyrians, the Phœnicians, and the Indo-Scythiac nations of Europe participated. They not only supported the propriety of the allegory, says Maurice, from the perfection of its external form, but fancifully extended the allusion to its interior composition, comparing the pure white shell to the fair expanse of heaven; the fluid, transparent white, to the circumambient air, and the more solid yolk to the central earth.

Even the Polynesians entertained the same general notions. The tradition of the Sandwich Islanders is that a bird (with them it is an emblem of Deity) laid an egg upon the waters which burst of itself and produced the Islands.

The great hermaphrodite first principle in its character of Unity, the Supreme Monad, the highest conception of Divinity was denominated Kneph or Cnuphis among the Egyptians. According to Plutarch this god was without beginning and without end, the One, uncreated and eternal, above all, and comprehending all. And as Brahm, "the Self-existent Incorruptible" Unity of the Hindus, by direction of His energetic will upon the expanse of chaos, "with a thought" (says Menu) produced a "golden egg blazing like a thousand stars," from which sprung Brahma, the Creator; so according to the mystagogues, Kneph, the Unity of Egypt, was represented as a serpent thrusting from his mouth an egg, from which proceeds the divinity Phtha, the active creative power, equivalent in all his attributes to the Indian Brahma.

That Kneph was symbolized by the ancient Egyptians under the form of serpent is well known. It is not, however, so well established that the act of creation was allegorically represented in Egypt by the symbolic serpent thrusting from its mouth an egg, although no doubt of the fact seems to have entertained by the various authors who have hitherto writtenon the Cosmogony and Mythology of the primitive nations of the East. With the view of ascertaining what new light has been thrown upon the subject by the investigations of the indefatigable Champollion and his followers---whose researches among the monuments and records of Ancient Egypt have been attended with most remarkable results---the following inquiries were addressed to Mr. G. R. Gliddon (U.S. Consul at Cairo), a gentleman distinguished for his acquaintance with Egyptian science, and his zeal in disseminating information on a subject too little understood:---

"Do the serpent and the egg, separate or in combination, occur among the Egyptian symbols and if they occur what significance seem to have been assigned them? Was the serpent in any way associated with the worship of the sun or the kindred worship of the Phallus?"

To these inquiries Mr. Gliddon replied as follows:---"In respect to your first inquiry; I concede at once that the general view of the Greco-Roman antiquity, the oriental traditions collected, often indiscriminately, by the Fathers and the concurring suffrages of all occidental Mythologists, attribute the compound symbol of the Serpent combined with the Mundane Egg to the Egyptians. Modern criticism however, coupled with the application of the test furnished by Champollion le-Jeune and his followers since 1827 to the hieroglyphics of Egypt, has recognised so many exotic fables and so much real ignorance of Egyptology in the accounts concerning that mystified country, handed down to us from the schools of Alexandria and Byzantium, that at the present hour science treads doubtingly, where but a few years ago it was fashionable to make the most sweeping assertions; and we now hesitate before qualifying, as Egyptian in origin, ideas that belong to the Mythologies of other eastern nations. Classical authority, correct enough when treating on the philosophy and speculative theories of Ptolemaic and Roman Alexandria, is generally at fault when in respect to questions belonging to anterior or Pharaonic times. Whatever we derive through the medium of the Alexandrines, and especially through their successors, the Gnostics, must by the Archæologist be received with suspicion.

After this you will not be surprised if I express doubts as to existence of the myth of the Serpent and Egg in the Cosmogony of the early Egyptians. It is lamentably true that, owing to twenty centuries of destruction, so fearfully wrought out by Mohammed Ali, we do not up to this day possess one tithe of the monuments or papyri bequeathed to posterity by the recording genius of the Khime. It is possible that this myth may have been contained in the vast amount of hieroglyphical literature now lost to us. But the fact that in no instance whatever, amid the myriads of inscribed or sculptured documents extant, does the symbol of the Serpent and the Egg occur, militates against the assumption of this, perhaps Phœnician myth, as originally Egyptian. "The worship of the Serpent," observes Ampêre, "by the Ophites may certainly have a real connection with the choice of the Egyptian symbol by which Divinity is designated in the paintings and hieroglyphics, and which is the Serpent Uræus (Basilisk royal, of the Greeks), the seraph set up by Moses. Se Ra Ph is the singular of seraphim, meaning Semiticé, splendour, fire, light; emblematic of the fiery disk of the sun and which, under the name of Nehushtan---"Serpent Dragon"---was broken up by the reforming Hezekiah (2 Kings, 18, 4); or with the serpent with wings and feet, which we see represented in the Funeral Rituals; but the serpent is everywhere in the Mythologies and Cosmogonies of the East, and we cannot be assured that the serpent of the Ophites (any more than that emitting or encircling the Mundane Egg) was Egyptian rather than Jewish, Persian, or Hindustanee."

"No serpents found in the hieroglyphics bear, so far as I can perceive, any direct relation to the Ouine Myth, nor have Egyptian Eggs any direct connection with the Cosmogonical Serpent. The egg, under certain conditions, seems to denote the idea of a human body. It is also used as a phonetic sign S, and when combined with T, is the determinative of the feminine gender; in which sense exclusively it is sometimes placed close to a serpent in hieroglyphical legends."

"My doubts apply in attempting to give a specific answer to you specific question; i.e., the direct connection, in Egyptian Mythology, of the Serpent and the Cosmogonical Egg. In the "Book of the Dead," according to a MS translation favoured me by the erudite Egyptologist, Mr. Birch, of the British Museum, allusion is made to the "great mundane egg" addressed by the deceased, which seems to refer to the winds or the atmosphere--- again the deceased exclaims 'I have raised myself up in the form of the great Hawk which comes out of the Egg (i.e., the Sun).'

"I do not here perceive any immediate allusion to the duplex emblem of the egg combined with the serpent, the subject of your query.

"Yet a reservation must be made in behalf of your very consistent hypothesis---supported, as I allow, by all oriental and classical authority, if not possibly by the Egyptian documents yet undeciphered---which hypothesis is Euclidean. 'Things which are equal to the same are equal to one another.' Now if the 'Mundane Egg' be in the papyric rituals the equivalent to Sun, and that by other hieroglyphical texts we prove the Sun to be, in Egypt as elsewhere, symbolized by the figure of a Serpent, does not the 'ultima ratio' resolve both emblems into one? Your grasp of this Old and New world Question reders it superfluous that I should now posite the syllogism. I content myself by referring you to the best of authorities. One point alone is what I would venture to suggest to your philosophical acumen, in respect to ancient 'parallelisms' between the metaphysical conceptions of radically distinct nations (if you please, 'species' of mankind, at geographically different centres of origins, compelled of necessity in ages anterior to alphabetical record to express their ideas by pictures, figurative or symbolical). It is that man's mind has always conceived, everywhere in the same method, everything that relates to him; because the inability in which his intelligence is circumscribed, to figure to his mind's eye existence distinct from his own, constrains him to devolve in the pictorial or sculptural delineation of his thoughts, within the same circle of ideas; and, ergo, the figurative representative of his ideas must ever be, in all ages and countries, the reflex of the same hypotheses, material or physical. May not the emblem of the Serpent and Egg, as well in the New as in the Old World, have originated from a similar organic law without thereby establishing intercourse? Is not your serpent a "rattle snake" and, ergo, purely American? Are not Egyptian Serpent all purely Nilotic? The metaphysical idea of the Cosmogonical Serpent may be one and the same; but does not the zoological diversity of representation prove that America, three thousand years ago, could have no possible intercourse with Egypt, Phœnicia, or vice versa?

"Such being the only values attached to Serpents and eggs in Egyptian hieroglyphics it is arduous to speculate whether an esoteric significance did or did not exist between those emblems in the, to us, unknown Cosmogony of the Theban and Memphite Colleges. I, too, could derive inferences and deduce analogies between the attributes of the God Knuphis, or the God Ptha, and the 'Mundane Egg' recorded by Eusebius, Jamblichus, and a wilderness of classical authorities, but I fear with no very satisfactory result. It is, however, due to Mr. Bonomi, to cite his language on this subject. Speaking of the colossal state of Rameses Sesostris at Metraheni, in a paper read before the Royal Society of Literature, London, June, 1845, he observes, 'There is one more consideration connected with the hieroglyphics of the great oval of the belt, though not affecting the preceding argument; it is the oval or egg which occurs between the figure of Ptha and the staff of which the usual signification is Son or Child, but which by a kind of two-fold meaning, common in the details of sculpture of this period (the 18th or 19th Dynasty, say B.C. 1500 or 1200), I am inclined to believe refers also to the myth or doctrine preserved in the writings of the Greek authors, as belonging to Vulcan and said to be derived from Egypt, viz., the doctrine of the Mundane Egg. Now, although in no Egyptian sculpture of the remote period of this statue has there been found any allusion to this doctrine, it is most distinctly hinted at in one of the age of the Ptolomies; and I am inclined to think it was imported from the Easy by Sesostris, where, in confirmation of its existence at a very remote period, I would quote the existence of those egg-shaped basaltic stones, embossed with various devices and covered with cuneatic inscriptions, which are brought from some of the ancient cities of Mesopotamia.

"In respect to your final inquiry, I may observe that I can produce nothing from the hieroglyphics to connect, directly, Phallic Worship with the solar emblem of the Serpent. In Semitic tongues, the same root signifies Serpent and Phallus; both in different senses are solar emblems."

In the Orphic Theogony a similar origin is ascribed to the egg, from which springs "the Egg-born Protogones," the Greek counterpart of the Egyptian Phtha. The egg in this instance also proceeds from the pre-eminent Unity, the Serpent God, the "Incomparable Cronus," or Hercules. (Bryant, quoting Athenagoras, observes---"Hercules was esteemed the chief god, the same as Cronus, and was said to have produced the Mundane Egg. He is represented in the Orphic Theology, under the mixed symbol of a lion and a serpent, and sometimes of a serpent only.")

Cronus was originally esteemed the Supreme, as is manifest from his being called Il or Ilus, which is the same with the Hebrew El and, according to St. Jerome, one of the ten names of God. Damascius, in the life of Isidorus, mentions distinctly that Cronus was worshipped under the name of El, who, according to Sanchoniathon, had no one superior or antecedent to himself.

Brahm, Cronus, and Kneph each represented the mystical union of the reciprocal or active and passive principles. Most, if not all, the primitive nations recognised this Supreme Unity, although they did not all assign him a name. He was the Creator of Gods, who were the Demiurgs of the Universe, the creators of all rational beings, angels and men, and the architects of the world.

The early writers exhaust language in endeavours to express the lofty character and attributes, and the superlative power and dignity of this great Unity, the highest conception of which man is capable. He is spoken of in the sacred book of the Hindus as the "Almighty, infinite, eternal, incomprehensible, self-existent Being; he who sees everything, though never seen; he who is not to be compassed by description; he from whom the universe proceeds; who reigns supreme, the light of all lights; whose power is too infinite to be imagined; is Brahm, the One Being, True and Unknown." (Coleman's Hind. Mythology.)

The supreme God of Gods of the Hindus was less frequently expressed by the name Brahm than by the mystical syllable O'M, which corresponded to the Hebrew Jehovah. Strange as the remark may seem to most minds, it is nevertheless true, that the fundamental principles of the Hindu religion were those of pure Monotheism, the worship of one supreme and only God. Brahm was regarded as too mighty to be named; and, while his symbolized or personified attributes were adored in gorgeous temples, not one was erected to him. The holiest verse of the Vedas is paraphrased as follows:

"Perfect truth; perfect happiness; without equal; immortal; absolute unity; whom neither speech can describe nor mind comprehend; all-pervading; all-transcending; delighted by his own boundless intelligence, not limited by space or time; without feet, moving swiftly; without hands, grasping all worlds; without ears, all-hearing, understanding all; without cause, the first of all causes; all-ruling; all-powerful; the Creator, Preserver, and Transformer of all things; such is the Great One, Brahm."

The character and power of Kneph are indicated in terms no less lofty and comprehensive than those applied to the omnipotent Brahm. He is described in the ancient Hermetic books as the "first God, immovable in the solitude of his Unity, the fountain of all things, the root of all primary, intelligble, existing forms, the God of Gods, before the etherial and empyrean Gods and the celestial."

In America this great Unity, this God of Gods, was equally recognised. In Mexico as Teotl, "he who is all in himself" (Tloque Nahuaque); in Peru as Varicocha, the "Soul of the Universe;" in Central America and Yucatan as Stunah Ku or Hunab Ku, "God of Gods, the incorporeal origin of all things." And as the Supreme Brahm of the Hindus, "whose name was unutterable," was worshipped under no external form and had neither temples nor altars erected to him, so the Supreme Teot and the corresponding Varicocha and Hunab Ku, "whose names," says the Spanish conquerors, "were spoken only with extreme dread," were without an image or an outward form of worship for the reason, according to the same authorities, that each was regarded as the Invisible and Unknown God.

The Mundane Egg, received as a symbol of original, passive, unorganized, formless nature, because associated, in conformity with primitive notions, with other symbols referring to the creative force or vitalizing influence. Thus in the Hindu cosmogony Brahma is represented, after long inertia, as arranging the passive elements, "creating the world and all visible things." Under the form of the emblematic bull the generative energy was represented breaking the quiescent egg. Encircled by the folds of the agatho-demon, a type of the active principle, it was suspended aloft at the temples of Tyre. For the serpent, like the bull, was an emblem of the sun or of the attributes of that luminary---itself the celestial emblem of the "Universal Father," the procreative power of nature. "Everywhere," says Faber, "we find the great father exhibiting himself in the form of a serpent, and everywhere we find the serpent invested with the attributes of the Great Father and partaking of the honours which were paid him." (Origin Pagan Idol., vol. I, p. 45).

Under this view, therefore, we may regard the compound symbol of the serpent and the egg, though specifically allusive to the general creation, as an illustration of the doctrine of the reciprocal principles which, as we have already seen, enters largely into the entire fabric of primitive philosophy and mythology.

Thus have we shewn that the grand conception of a Supreme Unity and the doctrine of the reciprocal principles existed in America in a well defined and easily recognised form.

Our present inquiry relates to the symbols by which they were represented in both continents. That these were not usually arbitrary, but resulted from associations, generally of an obvious kind, will be readily admitted.

CHAPTER V

That fire should be taken to be the physical, of what the sun is the celestial emblem, is sufficiently apparent; we can readily understand also how the bull, the goat, or ram, the phallus, and other symbols should have the same import; also how naturally and almost inevitably and universally the sun came to symbolize the active principle, the vivifying power, and how obviously the egg symbolized the passive elements of nature, but how the serpent came to possess, as a symbol, a like significance with these is not so obvious. That it did so, however, cannot be doubted, and the proofs will appear as we proceed; likewise that it sometimes symbolized the great hermaphrodite first principle, the Supreme Unity of the Greeks and Egyptians.

Although generally, it did not always symbolize the sun, or the power of which the sun is an emblem; but, invested with various meanings, it entered widely into the primitive mythologies. It typified wisdom, power, duration, the good and evil principles, life, reproduction---in short, in Egypt, Syria, Greece, India, China, Scandinavia, America, everywhere in the globe it has been a prominent emblem. In the somewhat poetical language of a learned author, "It entered into the mythology of every nation, consecrated almost every temple, symbolized almost every deity, was imagined in the heavens, stamped on the earth, and ruled in the realms of everlasting sorrow." Its general acceptance seems to have been remarked at a very early period. It arrested the attention of the ancient sages, who assigned a variety of reasons for its adoption, founded upon the natural history of the reptile. Among these speculations, none are more curious than those preserved by Sanchoniathon, who says:---"Taut first attributed something of the Divine nature to the Serpent, in which he was followed by the Phœnicians and Egyptians. For this animal was esteemed by him to be the most inspirited of all reptiles, and of a fiery nature, inasmuch as it exhibits an incredible celerity, moving by its spirit, without hands or feet, or any of the external members by which the other animals effect their motion: and, in its progress, it assumes a variety of forms, moving in a spiral course, and darting forward with whatever degree of swiftness it pleases."

It is, moreover, long lived, and has the quality not only of putting off its old age, and assuming a second youth, but of receiving at the same time an augmentation of its size and strength; and when it has filled the appointed measure of its existence, it consumes itself, as Taut has laid down in the Sacred Books, upon which account this animal is received into the sacred rites and mysteries.

Horapollo, referring to the serpent symbol, says of it:---"When the Egyptians would represent the Universe they delineate a serpent bespeckled with variegated scales, devouring its own tail, the scales intimating the stars in the Universe. The animal is extremely heavy, as is the earth, and extremely slippery like the water, moreover, it every year puts off its old age with its skin, as in the Universe the annual period effects a corresponding change and becomes renovated, and the making use of its own body for food implies that all things whatever, which are generated by divine providence in the world, undergo a corruption into them again."

Nothing is more certain than that the serpent at a very remote period was regarded with high veneration as the most mysterious of living creatures. Its habits were imperfectly understood, and it was invested, as we perceive from the above quotations, with the most extraordinary qualities. Alike the object of fear, admiration, and wonder, it is not surprising that it became early connected with man's superstitions, but how it obtained so general a predominance it is difficult to understand.

Perhaps there is no circumstance in the natural history of the serpent more striking than that alluded to by Sanchoniathon, viz.: the annual sloughing of its skin, or supposed rejuvenation.

"As an old serpent casts his scaly vest,
Wreaths in the Sun, in youthful glory dressed,
So when Alcides' mortal mould resign'd,

His better part enlarged, and grew refin'd."---Ovid.

It was probably this which connected it with the idea of an eternal succession of forms, constant reproduction and dissolution, a process which was supposed by the ancients to have been for ever going on in nature. This doctrine is illustrated in the notion of a succession of Ages which prevailed among the Greeks, corresponding to the Yugs of the Hindus, and Suns of the aboriginal Mexicans. It is further illustrated by the annual dissolution and renovation exhibited in the succession of the seasons, and which was supposed to result from the augmentation and decline of the active principle, the Sun.

The mysteries of Osiris, Isis, and Horus, in Egypt; Atys and Cybéle, in Phrygia; Ceres and Proserpine, at Eleusis; of Venus and Adonis in Phœnicia; of Bona Dea, and Priapus, in Rome, are all susceptible of one explanation. They all set forth and illustrated, by solemn and impressive rites and mystical symbols, the grand phenomena of nature, especially as connected with the creation of things and the perpetuation of life. In all, it is worthy of remark, the serpent was more or less conspicuously introduced, always as symbolical of the invigorating or active energy of nature. In the mysteries of Ceres and Proserpine, the grand secret communicated to the initiated was thus enigmatically expressed: Taurus Draconem genuit, et Taurum Draco; "The bull has begotten a serpent, and the serpent a bull." The bull, as already seen, was a prominent emblem of generative force, the Bacchus Zagreus, or Tauriformis.

The doctrine of an unending succession of forms was not remotely connected with that of regeneration, or new birth, which was part of the phallic system, and which was recognised in a form more or less distinct in nearly all the primitive religions. In Hindustan, this doctrine is still enforced in the most unequivocal manner, through the medium of rites of portentous solemnity and significance to the devotees of the Hindu religion. "For the purpose of regeneration," says Wilford, "it is directed to make an image of pure gold of the female powers of nature in the shape of either a woman or a cow. In this statue the person to be regenerated is enclosed, and afterwards dragged out through the usual channel. As a statue of pure gold, and of proper dimensions would be too expensive, it is sufficient to make an image of the sacred Yoni, through which the person to be regenerated is to pass.

We have seen the serpent as a symbol of productive energy associated with the egg as a symbol of the passive elements of nature. The egg does not, however, appear except in the earlier cosmogonies. "As the male serpent," says Faber, "was employed to symbolize the Great Father, so the female serpent was equally used to typify the Great Mother. Such a mode of representation may be proved by express testimony, and is wholly agreeable to the analogy of the entire system of Gentile mythology. In the same manner that the two great parents were worshipped under the hieroglyphics of a bull and cow, a lion and lioness, &c., so they were adored under the cognate figures of a male and female serpent."

Nearly every enquirer into the primitive superstitions of men has observed a close relationship, if not an absolute identity, in what are usually distinguished as Solar, Phallic, and Serpent Worship, yet the rationale of the connection has been rarely detected. They really are all forms of a single worship. "If (as it seems certain) they all three be identical," observes Mr. O'Brien, "where is the occasion for surprise at our meeting the sun, phallus, and serpent, the constituent symbols of each, occurring in combination, embossed upon the same table, and grouped upon the same architrave."

We turn again to America. The principal God of the Aztecs, subordinate to the great Unity, was the impersonation of the active, creative energy, Tezcatilopoca or Tonacatlecoatl. He was also called Tonacateuctli.

Like the Hindu Brahma, the Greek Phanes, and the Egyptian Phtha, he was the "Creator of heaven and earth," "the Great Father," "the God of Providence," who dwells in heaven, earth, and hades, and attends to the government of the world. To denote this unfailing power and eternal youth, his figure was that of a young man. His celestial emblem was Tonatiuh, the Sun. His companion or wife was Cihuacohuatl or Tonaeacihua, "the Great Mother" both of gods and men.

The remaining gods and goddesses of the Aztec Pantheon resolve themselves into modified impersonations of these two powers. Thus, we have Ometuctli and Omecihuatl, the adorable god and goddess who preside over the celestial paradise, and which, though generally supposed to be distinct divinities, are, nevertheless, according to the Codex Vaticanus, but other names for the deities already designated. We have also Xiuhteuctli, "Master of the Year," "the God of Fire," the terrestrial symbol of the active principle, and Xochitli, "the Goddess of Earth and Corn;" Tlaloc and Cinteotl, or Chalchiuhcueije, "the god and goddess of the waters;" Mictlanteuctli and Mictlancihuatl, "the god and goddess of the dead;" the terrible Mexitli or Huitzlipochtli, corresponding to the Hindu Siva, in his character of destroyer, and his wife Teoyamiqui, whose image, like that of Kali, the consort of Siva, was decorated with the combined emblems of life and death.

In the simple mythology and pure Sabianism of Peru, we have already shown the existence of the primeval principles symbolized, the first by the Sun and the second by his wife and sister the Moon. That the sun was here regarded as symbolizing the intermediate father, or demiurgic creator, cannot be doubted. The great and solemn feast of Raimi was instituted in acknowledgment of the Sun as the great father of all visible things, by whom all living things are generated and sustained. The ceremonies of this feast were emblematical, and principally referred to the sun as the reproductive and preserving power of nature. In Mexico, where the primitive religion partook of the fiercer nature of the people, we find the Raimaic ceremonies assuming a sanguinary character, and the acknowledgment of the reproductive associated with the propitiation of its antagonist principle, as we see in the orgies of Huitzlipochtli in his character of the Destroyer. The same remarks hold true of Central America, the religion and mythology of which country correspond essentially with those of the nations of Anahuac.

We have said that the principal god of the Aztec pantheon, subordinate only to the Unity and corresponding to the Hindu Brahma, was Tezcatlipoea, Tonacatlecoalt, or Tonacateuctli. If we consult the etymology of these names we shall find ample confirmation of the correctness of the deductions already drawn from the mythologies of the East. Thus Tonacateuctli embodied Lord Sun from Tonatiuh, Sun, nacayo or catl, body or person, and teuctli, master or lord. Again, Tonacatlcoatl, the Serpent Sun, from Tonctiah and catl, as above, and coatl, serpent. If we adopt another etymology for the names (and that which seems to have been most generally accepted by the early writers) we shall have Tonacateuctli, Lord of our Flesh, from to, the possessive pronoun plural, nacatl, flesh or body, and teuctli, master or lord. We shall also have Tonacatlecoatl, Serpent of our Flesh, from to, and nacatl, and coatl, serpent.

According to Sahagim, Tezcatlipoca, in his character of the God of Hosts, was addressed as follows by the Mexican High Priest:---"We entreat that those who die in war may be received by thee, our Father the Sun, and our Mother the Earth, for thou alone reignest." The same authority informs us that in the prayer of thanks, returned to Tezcatlipoca by the Mexican kings on the occasion of their coronation, God was recognised as the God of fire, to whom Xiuthteuctli, Lord of Vegetation, and specifically Lord of Fire, bears the same relation that Suyra does to the first person of the Hindu Triad. The king petitions that he may act "in conformity with the will of the ancient God, the Father of all Gods, who is the God of Fire; whose habitation is in the midst of the waters, encompassed by battlements, surrounded by rocks as it were with roses, whose name is Xiuteuctli," etc.

Tonacateuctli, or Tezcatlipoca, is often, not to say generally, both on the monuments and in the paintings, represented as surrounded by a disc of the sun.

The name of the primitive goddess, the wife of Tezcatlipoca, was Cihuacohuatl or Tonacacihua. She was well known by other names, all referring to her attributes. The etymology of Cihuacohuatl is clearly Cihua, woman or female, and coatl, serpent---Female Serpent. And Tonacacihua is Female Sun, from Tonatiuh nacatl (as before) and cihua, woman or female. Adopting the other etymology, it is Woman of our Flesh.

Gama, who is said to be by far the most intelligent author who has treated with any detail of the Mexican Gods, referring to the serpent symbols belonging to the statue of Teoyaomiqui, says---"These refer to another Goddess named Cihuacohuatl, or Female Serpent, which the Mexicans believe gave to the light, at a single birth, two children, one male and the other female, to whom they refer the origin of mankind; and hence twins, among the Mexicans, are called cohuatl or coatl, which is corrupted in the pronunciation by the vulgar into coate."

Whichever etymology we assign to Tonaca in these combinations, the leading fact that the Great Father was designated as the male serpent, and the Great Mother as the female serpent, remains unaffected. Not only were they thus designated, but Cinacoatl or Cihuacohuatl was generally if not always represented, in the paintings, accompanied by a great snake or featherheaded serpent (Tonacatlecoatl "serpent sun") in which the monkish interpreters did not fail to discover a palpable allusion to Eve and the tempter of the garden.

Pursuing the subject of the connection of the Serpent Symbol with American Mythology, we remark the fact that it was a conspicuous symbol and could not escape the attention of the most superficial of observers of the Mexican and Central American monuments, and mythological paintings. The early Spaniards were particularly struck with its prominence.

"The snake," says Dupaix, "was a conspicuous object in the Mexican mythology, and we find it carved in various shapes and sizes, coiled, extended, spiral or entwined with great beauty, and sometimes represented with feathers and other ornaments. These different representatives," he continues, "no doubt denoted its different attributes."

The editor of Kingsborough's great work observes:---"Like the Egyptian Sphynx, the mystical snake of the Mexicans had its enigmas, and both are beyond our power to unravel;" this, however, is a matter of opinion, and the conclusion is one from which many will strongly dissent.

In almost every primitive mythology we find, not only a Great Father and Mother, the representatives of the reciprocal principles, and a Great Hermaphrodite Unity from whom the first proceed and in whom they are both combined, but we find also a beneficial character, partaking of a divine and human nature, who is the Great Teacher of Men, who instructs them in religion, civil organization and the arts, and who, after a life of exemplary usefulness, disappears mysteriously, leaving his people impressed with the highest respect for his institutions and the profoundest regard for his memory. This demi-god, to whom divine honours are often paid after his withdrawal from the earth, is uaually the Son of the Sun, or of the Demiurgic Creator, the Great Father, who stands at the head of the primitive pantheons and subordinate only to the Supreme Unity; he is born of an earthly mother, a virgin, and often a vestal of the Sun, who conceives in a mysterious manner, and who, after giving birth to her half-divine son, is herself sometimes elevated to the rank of goddess. In the more refined and systematized mythologies he appears clearly as an incarnation of the Great Father and partaking of his attributes, his terrestial representative, and the mediator between him and man. He appears as Buddha in India; Fohi in China; Schaka in Thibet; Zoroasta in Persia; Osiris in Egypt; Taut in Phœnicia; Hermes or Cadmus in Greece; Romulus in Rome; Odin in Scandinavia; and in each case is regarded as the Great Teacher of Men, and the founder of religion.

In the mythological systems of America, this intermediate demi-god was not less clearly recognised than in those of the Old World; indeed, as these systems were less complicated because less modified from the original or primitive forms, the Great Teacher appears here with more distinctness. Among the savage tribes his origin and character were, for obvious reasons, much confused; but among the more advanced nations he occupied a well defined position.

Among the nations of Anahuac, he bore the name of Quetzalcoatl (Feathered Serpent) and was regarded with the highest veneration. His festivals were the most gorgeous of the year. To him it is said the great temple of Cholula was dedicated. His history, drawn from various sources, is as follows:---The god of the "Milky Way"---in other words, of Heaven---the principal deity of the Aztec Pantheon, and the Great Father of gods and men, sent a message to a virgin of Tulan, telling her that it was the will of the gods that she should conceive a son, which she did without knowing any man. This son was Quetzalcoatl, who was figured as tall, of fair complexion, open forehead, large eyes and a thick beard. He became high priest of Tulan, introduced the worship of the gods, established laws displaying the profoundest wisdom, regulated the calendar, and maintained the most rigid and exemplary manners in his life. He was averse to cruelty, abhorred war, and taught men to cultivate the soil, to reduce metal from their ores, and many other things necessary to their welfare. Under his benign administration the widest happiness prevailed amongst men. The corn grew to such a size that a single ear was a load for a man; gourds were as long as a man's body; it was unnecessary to dye cotton for it grew of all colours; all fruits were in the greatest profusion and of extraordinary size; there were also vast numbers of beautiful and sweet singing birds. His reign was the golden age of Anahuac. He however disappeared suddenly and mysteriously, in what manner is unknown. Some say he died on the sea-horse, and others say that he wandered away in search of the imaginary kingdom of Tlallapa. He was deified; temples were erected to him, and he was adorned throughout Anahuac.

Quetzalcoatl is, therefore, but an incarnation of the "Serpent Sun" Tonacatlecoalt, and, as is indicated by his name, the feathered serpent was his recognised symbol. He was thus symbolized in accordance with a practice which (says Gama) prevailed in Mexico, of associating or connecting with the representatives of a god or goddess, the symbols of the other deities from whom they are derived, or to whom they sustain some relation. His temples were distinguished as being circular, and the one dedicated to his worship in Mexico, was, according to Gomera, entered by a door "like unto the mouth of a serpent, which was a thing to fear by those who went in thereat, especially by the Christians, to whom it represented very hell."

The Mayas of Yucatan had a demi-god corresponding entirely with Quetzalcoatl, if he was not the same under a different name---a conjecture very well sustained by the evident relationship between the Mexican and Mayan mythologies. He was named Itzamna or Zamna, and was the only son of the principal God, Kinchanan. He arrived from the East, and instructed the people in all that was essential to their welfare. "He," says Cogolludo, "invented the characters which they use as letters, and which are called after him, Itzamna, and they adore him as a god."

There was another similar character in Yucatan, called Ku Kulcan or Cuculcan, another in Nicaragua named Theotbilake, son of their principal god Thomathoyo, and another in Colombia bearing the name of Bochia. Peru and Guatemala furnish similar traditions, as do also Brazil, the nations of the Tamanac race, Florida, and various savage tribes of the West.

The serpent, as we show elsewhere, was an emblem both of Quetzalcoatl and of Ku Kulcan---a fact which gives some importance to the statement of Cabrera that Votan of Guatemala as above was represented to be a serpent, or of serpent origin.

Torquemada states that the images of Huitzlipochtli of Mexico, Quetzalcoatl, and Tlaloc were each represented with a golden serpent, bearing different symbolical sacrificial allusions. He also assures us that serpents often entered into the symbolical sacrificial ceremonies of the Mexicans, and presents the following example:---

"Among the many sacrifices which these Indians made, there was one which they performed in honour of the mountains, by forming serpents out of wood or of the roots of the trees, to which they affixed serpents' heads, and also dolls of the same, which they called Ecatotowin, which figures of serpents and fictitious children they covered with dough, named by them Tzoalli, composed of the seeds of Bledos, and placed them on supports of wood, carved in the representation of hills or mountains, on the tops of which they fixed them. This was the kind of offering which they made to the mountains and high hills.

The mother of Huitzlipochtli was a priestess of Tezcatlipoca (a cleanser of the temple, says Gama) named Coatlantona, Coatlcué, or Coatlcyue (serpent of the temple or serpent woman). She was extremely devoted to the gods, and one day when walking in the temple, she beheld, descending in the air, a ball made of variously coloured feathers. She placed it in her girdle, became at once pregnant, and afterwards was delivered of Mexith or Huitzlipochtli, full armed, with a spear in one hand, a shield in the other, and a crest of green feathers on his head. He became, according to some, their leader into Anahuac, guiding them to the place where Mexico is built. His statue was of gigantic size, and covered with ornaments each one of which had its significance. He was depicted placed upon a seat, from the four corners of which issued four large serpents. "His body," says Gomeza, "was beset with pearls, precious stones and gold, and for collars and chains around his neck ten hearts of men made of gold. It had also a counterfeit vizard, with eyes of glass, and in its neck death painted, all of which things had their considerations and meanings." It was to him in his divine character of the destroyer that the bloodiest sacrifices of Mexico were performed. His wife, Teoyaomiqui (from Teo, sacred or divine; Yaoyotl, war; and Miqui, to kill) was represented as a figure bearing the full breats of a woman, literally enveloped in serpents, and ornamented with feathers, shells, and the teeth and claws of a tiger. She had a necklace composed of six hands. Around her waist is a belt to which death's heads are attached. One of her statues, a horrible figure, still exists in the city of Mexico. It is carved from a solid block of basalt, and is nine feet in height and five and a half in breadth.

It is not improbable that the serpent-mother of Huitzlipochti was an impersonation of the great female serpent Cinacohuatl, the wife of Tonacatlecoatl, the serpent-father of Quetzalcoatl. However this may be, it is clear that a more intimate connection exists between the several principal divinities of Mexico, than appears from the confused and meagre accounts which have been left us of their mythology. Indeed, we have seen that the Hindu Triad, Brahma, Vishnu, and Siva, has very nearly its counterpart in Tezcatlipoca, Tlaloc, and the celestial Huitzlipochtli, the Creator, Preserver, and Destroyer and Reproducer. In the delineations of Siva or Mahadeo, in his character of the destroyer, he is represented as wrapped in tiger skins. A hooded snake is twisted around him and lifts its head above his shoulder, and twisted snakes form his head-dress. In other cases he holds a spear, a sword, a serpent, and a skull, and has a girdle of skulls around his waist. The bull Nandi (emblem of generative force), as also the lingham, are among his emblems. To him were dedicated the bloodiest sacrifices of India. Durga, or Kali (an impersonation of Bhavin, goddess of nature and fecundity) corresponds with the Mexican Tesyaomiqui, and is represented in a similar manner. She is a war goddess and her martial deeds give her a high position in the Hindu pantheon. As Kali, her representatives are most terrible. The emblems of destruction are common to all; she is entwined with serpents; a circlet of flowers surrounds her head; a necklace of skulls; a girdle of dissevered human hands; tigers crouching at her feet---indeed every combination of the horrible and the loathsome is invoked to portray the dark character which she represents. She delights in human sacrifices and the ritual prescribes that, previous to the death of the victim, she should be invoked as follows: "Let the sacrificer first repeat the name of Kali thrice, Hail, Kali! Kali! Hail, Devi! Hail, Goddess of Thunder! iron-sceptered, hail, fierce Kali! Cut, slay, destroy! bind, secure! Cut with the axe, drink blood, slay, destroy!" "She has four hands," says Patterson, "two of which are employed in the destruction which surrounds her, and the other upwards, which seems to promise the regeneration of nature by a new creation. "On her festivals," says Coleman, "her temples literally stream with blood." As Durga, however, she is often represented as the patroness of Virtue and her battles with evil demons form the subject of many Hindu poems. She is under this aspect the armed Phallas.

We have seen that the Creator of the World, the Great Father of the Aztecs, Tonacatlecoatl or Tezcatlipoca, and his wife Cihuacohuatl, were not only symbolized as the Sun and Moon, but also that they were designated as the male and female serpent, and that in the mythological pictures the former was represented as a feather-headed snake. We have also seen that the incarnate or human representative of this deity Quetzalcoatl, was also symbolized as a feathered serpent. This was in accordance with the system of the Aztecs, who represented cognate symbols, and invested the impersonations or descendants of the greater gods with their emblems.

These facts being well established, many monuments of American antiquity, otherwise inexplicable, become invested with significance. In Mexico, unfortunately, the monumental records of the ancient inhabitants have been so ruthlessly destroyed or obliterated that now they afford us but little aid in our researches. Her ancient paintings, although there are some which have escaped the general devastation, are principally beyond our reach and cannot be consulted particularly upon these points. In Central America, however, we find many remains which, although in a ruined state, are much more complete and much more interesting than any others concerning which we possess any certain information.

The researches and explorations of Messrs. Stephens and Catherwood have placed many of these before us in a form which enables us to detect their leading features. Ranking first among the many interesting groups of ruins discovered by these gentlemen, both in respect to their extent and character, are those of Chichen-itza. One of the structures comprising this group is described as follows:---"The building called the Castillo is the first which we saw, and is, from every point of view, the grandest and most conspicuous object that towers above the plain. The mound upon which it stands measures one hundred and ninety-seven feet at the base, and is built up, apparently solid, to the height of seventy-five feet. On the west side is a stairway thirty-seven feet wide; on the north another, forty-four feet wide, and containing ninety steps. On the ground at the foot of the stairway, forming a bold, striking, and well-conceived commencement, are two colossal serpents' heads (feathered) ten feet in length, with mouths wide open and tongues protruding."

"No doubt they were emblematic of some relgious belief, and, in the minds of the imaginative people passing between them, must have excited feelings of solemn awe. The platform on the mound is about sixty feet square and is crowned by a building measuring forty-three by forty-nine feet. Single doorways face the east, south and west, having massive lentils of zapote wood, covered with elaborate carvings, and the jambs are ornamented with sculptured figures. The sculpture is much worn, but the head-dress of feathers and portions of the rich attire still remain. The face is well preserved, and has a dignified aspect. All the other jambs are decorated with sculptures of the same general character, and all open into a corridor six feet wide, extending around three sides of the building. The interior of this building was ornamented with very elaborate but much obliterated carvings.

"The sacred character of this remarkable structure is apparent at the first glance, and it is equally obvious that the various sculptures must have some significance. The entrance between the two colossal serpents' heads remind us at once of Gomera's description of the entrance to the temple of Quetzalcoatl in Mexico, which 'was like unto the mouth of a serpent and which was a thing to fear by those who entered in thereat.'"

The circumstance that these heads are feathered seems further to connect this temple with the worship of that divinity. But in the figures sculptured upon the jambs of the entrances, and which, Mr. Stephens observes, were of the same general character throughout, we have further proof that this structure was dedicated to a serpent divinity. Let it be remembered that the dignified personage there represented is accompanied by a feathered serpent, the folds of which are gracefully arrayed behind the figure and the tail of which is marked by the rattles of the rattle-snake---the distinguishing mark of the monumental serpent of the continent, whether represented in the carvings of the mounds or in the sculptures of Central America. This temple, we may therefore reasonably infer, was sacred to the benign Quetzalcoatl, or a character corresponding to him, whose symbolical serpent guarded the ascent to the summit, and whose imposing representations was sculptured on its portals. This inference is supported by the fact that in Mexican paintings the temples of Quetzalcoatl are indicated by a serpent entwined around or rising above them, as may be seen in an example from the Codex Borgianus in Kingsborough.

But this is not all. We have already said that amongst the Itzaes---"holy men"---the founders of Chichen-itza and afterwards of Mayapan, there was a character, corresponding in many respects with Quetzalcoatl, named Ku Kulcan or Cuculcan. Torquemada, quoted by Cogolludo, asserts that this was but another name for Quetzalcoatl. Cogolludo himself speaks of Ku Kulcan as "one who had been a great captain among them," and was afterwards worshipped as a god. Herrara states that he ruled at Chichen-itza; that all agreed that he came from the westward, but that a difference exists as to whether he came before or afterwards or with the Itzaes. "But," he adds, "the name of the structure at Chichen-itza and the events of that country after the death of the lords, shows that Cuculcan governed with them. He was a man of good disposition, not known to have had wife or children, a great statesman, and therefore looked upon as a god, he having contrived to build another city in which business might be managed. To this purpose they pitched upon a spot eight leagues from Merida, where they made an enclosure of about eighth of a league in circuit, being a wall of dry stone with only two gates. They built temples, calling the greatest of them Cuculcan. Near the enclosures were the houses of the prime men, among whom Cuculcan divided the land, appointing towns to each of them.

"This city was called Mayapan (the standard of Maya), the Mayan being the language of the country. Cuculcan governed in peace and quietness and with great justice for some years, when, having provided for his departure and recommended to them the good form of government which had been established, he returned to Mexico the same way he came, making some stay at Chanpotan, where, as a memorial of his journey, he erected a structure in the sea, which is to be seen to this day." [1]

We have here the direct statement that the principal structure at Mayapan was called Cuculcan; and from the language of Herrara the conclusion is irresistible that the principal structure of Chichen-itza was also called by the same name. These are extremely interesting facts, going far to show what the figure represented in the "Castillo," and which we have identified upon other evidence as being that of a personage corresponding to Quetzalcoatl, is none other than the figure of the demi-god Ku Kulcan, or Cuculcan, to whose worship the temple was dedicated and after whom it was named.

If we consult the etymology of the name Ku Kulcan we shall have further and striking evidence in support of this conclusion. Ku in the Mayan language means God, and can serpent. We have, then, Ku Kulcan, God---Kul, Serpent, or Serpent-God. What Kul signifies it is not pretended to say, but we may reasonably conjecture, that it is a qualifying word to can serpent. Kukum is feather, and it is possible that by being converted into an adjective form it may change its termination into Kukul. The etymology may therefore be Kukumcan Feather-Serpent, or Kukulcan Feathered Serpent. We, however, repose on the first explanation, and unhesitatingly hazard the opinion that, when opportunity is afforded of ascertaining the value of Kul, the correctness of our conclusions will be fully justified.

---

[1] Herrara, Hist. America, vol. iv., pp. 162-3

And here we may also add that the etymology of Kinchahan, the name of the principal god of the Mayas and corresponding to Tonacatlcoatl of Mexico, is precisely the same as that of the latter. Kin is Sun in the Mayan language, and Chahan, as every one acquainted with the Spanish pronunciation well knows, is nothing more than a variation in orthography for Cään or Can, serpent. Kin Chahan, Kincaan, or Kincan is, therefore, Sun-serpent.

The observation that Quetzalcoatl might be regarded as the incarnation of Tezcatlipoca, or Tonacatlcoatl, corresponding to the Buddha of the Hindus, was based upon the coincidences in their origin, character, and teachings, but there are some remarkable coincidences between the temples dedicated to the worship of these two great teachers---or perhaps we should say, between the religious structures of Central America and Mexico and Hindustan and the islands of the Indian Archipelago, which deserve attention.

From the top of the lofty temple at Chichen-itza, just described, Mr. Stephans saw, for the first time, groups of columns or upright stones which, he observes, proved upon examination to be among the most remarkable and unitelligible remains he had yet encountered. "They stood in rows of three, four and five abreast, many rows continuing in the same direction, when they collectively changed and pursued another. They were low, the tallest not more than six feet high. Many had fallen, in some places lying prostrate in rows, all in the same direction, as if thrown intentionally. In some cases, they extended to the bases of large mounds, on which were ruins of buildings and large fragments of sculptures, while in others they branched off and terminated abruptly. I counted three hundred and eighty, and there were many more; but so many were broken and lay so irregularly that I gave up counting them."

Those represented by Mr. Stephens, in his plate, occur in immediate connection with the temple above described, and enclose an area nearly four hundred feet square.

In the third volume of the "Transactions of the Royal Asiatic Society" is an account of the mixed temples of the ancient city of Anarajapura (situated in the centre of the island of Ceylon) by Captain Chapman, of the British Army. The remarkable character of these ancient structures and the decided resemblances which they sustain to those in Central America, and particularly to the group of Chichen-itza, justify a somewhat detailed notice of them.

According to native records, Anarajapura was, for a period of thirteen hundred years, both the principal seat of the religion of the country and residence of its kings. It abounded in magnificent buildings, sculptures, and other works of art, and was, as it still is, held in the greatest veneration by the followers of Buddha as the most sacred spot in the island.

"At this time," says Captain Chapman, "the only remaining traces of the city consist of nine temples; of two very extensive banks; of several smaller ones in ruins; of groups of pillars, and of portions of walls, which are scattered over an extent of several miles. The nine temples are still held in great reverence, and are visited periodically by the Buddhists. They consist of first of an enclosure, in which are the sacred trees called the Bogaha; the Thousand Pillars called Lowá Mahá Payá; and the seven mounds or Dagobas, each one of which has a distinct name given it by its founder."

The temple of Bo Malloa, especially sacred to Buddha, is of granite and consists of a series of four rectangular terraces, faced with granite, rising out of each other and diminishing both in height and extent, upon which are situated the altars and the sacred Bogaha trees, or trees of Buddha. The total height of the terraces is about twenty feet and the extent of the largest thirty paces by fifteen. These terraces are ascended by flights of steps. At the foot of the principal flight are slabs of granite, placed perpendicularly, upon which figures are boldly sculptured; and between is a semi-circular stone with simple mouldings let in the ground. Upon the east of the building projects a colossal figure of Buddha. Another similar, but smaller, structure is placed a little to the eastward of that first described. Both are surrounded by a wall, enclosing a space one hundred and twenty-five paces long by seventy-five wide, within which are planted a variety of odoriferous trees.

A few paces to the eastward of this enclosure are the ruins of the "Thousand Pillars." These consisted originally of 1600 pillars, disposed in a square. The greater part are still standing; they consist, with a few exceptions, of a single piece of gneiss in the rough state in which they were quarried. They are ten or twelve feet above the ground; twelve inches by eight square, and about four feet from each other; but the two in the centre of the outer line differ from the rest in being of hard blue granite, and in being more carefully finished. These pillars were said to have been covered with chunam (plaster) and thus converted into columns having definite forms and proportions. There is a tradition that there was formerly in the centre of this square a brazen chamber, in which was contained a relic held in much veneration. A few paces from this was a single pillar of gneiss in a rough state, which was from fourteen to sixteen feet high.

Captain Chapman observes that structures, accompanied by similar groups of columns, exist on the opposite or continental coast. The temples of Rámiseram, Madura, and the celebrated one of Seringham, have each their "Thousand Pillars." In Rámiseram the pillars are arranged in colonnades of several parallel rows, and these colonnades are separated by tanks or spaces occupied by buildings in the manner indicated by Mr. Stephans at Chichen-itza. Some of these pillars are carved; others are in their rough state or covered with plaster. In Madura the pillars are disposed in a square of lines radiating in such a manner that a person placed in the centre can see through in every direction. This square is on a raised terrace, the pillars rude and only about eight feet high. At Seringham the pillars also form a square.

The dagobas, occurring in connection with the temple of Buddha and the "Thousand Pillars" at Anarájapura, deserve a notice, as they correspond in many respects with some of the structures at Chichen. They are of various dimensions and consist generally of raised terraces or platforms of great extent, surrounded by mounds of earth faced with brick or stone, and often crowned with circular, dome-shaped structures. The base is usually surrounded by rows of columns. They vary from fifty to one hundred and fifty feet in height. The dagobas, of intermediate size, have occasionally a form approaching that of a bubble, but in general they have the form of a bell. They constitute part of the Buddhist Temples, almost without exception. We have, in the character of these singular columns and their arrangement in respect to each other and the pyramidal structures in connection with which they are found, a most striking resemblance between the ruins of Chichen-itza in Central America, and Anarájapura in Ceylon---between the temples of Buddha and those of Quetzalcoatl, or some corresponding character. The further coincidences which exist between the sacred architecture of India and Central America will be reserved for another place. We cannot, however, omit to notice here the structure at Chichen-itza designated as the "Caracol," both from its resemblance to the dagobas of Ceylon and its connection with the worship of the Serpent Deity. Mr. Stephens describes it as follows:---

"It is circular in form and is known by the name of the Caracol, or Winding Staircase, on account of its interior arrangements. It stands on the upper of two terraces. The lower one measuring in front, from north to south, two hundred and twenty three feet, and is still in good preservation. A grand staircase, forty-five feet wide, and containing twenty steps, rises to the platform of this terrace. On each side of the staircase, forming a sort of balustrade, rest the entwined bodies of two gigantic serpents, three feet wide, portions of which are still in place; and amongst the ruins of the staircase a gigantic head, which had terminated, at one side the foot of the steps. The platform of the second terrace measured eighty feet in front and fifty-five in depth, and is reached by another staircase forty-two feet wide and having forty-two steps. In the centre of the steps and against the wall of the terrace are the remains of a pedestal six feet high, on which probably once stood an idol. On the platform, fifteen feet from the last step, stands the building. It is twenty-two feet in diameter and has four small doorways facing the cardinal points. Above the cornice the roof sloped off so as to form an apex. The height, including the terraces, is little short of sixty feet. The doorways gave entrance to a circular corridor five feet wide. The inner wall has four doorways, smaller than the others, and standing intermediately with respect to them. These doors give entrance to a second circular corridor, four feet wide, and in the centre is a circular mass, apparently of solid stone, seven feet six inches in diameter; but in one place, at the height of eleven feet from the floor, was a small square-opening, which I endeavoured to clear out but without success. The roof was so tottering that I could not discover to what this opening led. The walls of both corridors were plastered and covered with paintings, and both were covered with a triangular arch."

Mr. Stephens also found at Mayapan, which city, as we have seen, was built by Ku Kulcan, the great ruler and demi-god of Chichen-itza, a dome-shaped edifice of much the same character with that here described. It is the principal structure here, and stands on a mound thirty feet high. The walls are ten feet high to the top of the lower cornice, and fourteen more to the upper one. It has a single entrance towards the west. The outer wall is five feet thick, within which is a corridor three feet wide, surrounding a solid cylindrical mass of stone, nine feet in thickness. The walls have four or five coats of stucco and were covered with remains of paintings, in which red, yellow, blue and white were distinctly visible. On the south-west of the building was a double row of columns, eight feet apart, though probably from the remains around, there had been more, and by clearing away the trees others might be found. They were two feet and a half in diameter. We are not informed upon the point but presumably the columns were arranged, in respect to the structure, in the same manner as those accompanying the dagobas in Ceylon, or the mounds of Chichen-itza.

Among the ruins of Chichen are none more remarkable than that called by the natives "Egclesia" or the Church. It is described by Mr. Stephens as consisting of "two immense parallel walls each two hundred and seventy-five feet long, thirty feet thick, and placed one hundred and twenty feet apart. One hundred feet from the northern extremity, facing the space between the walls, stands, on a terrace, a building thirty-five feet long, containing a single chamber, with the front fallen, and rising among the rubbish the remains of two columns elaborately ornamented, the whole interior wall being exposed to view, covered from top to bottom with sculptured figures in bas-relief much worn and faded. At the southern end also, placed back a hundred feet and corresponding in position, is another building eighty-one feet long, in ruins, but also exhibiting the remains of this column richly sculptured. In the centre of the great stone walls, exactly opposite each other, and at the height of thirty feet from the ground, are two massive stone rings, four feet in diameter and one foot one inch thick, the diameter of the hole is one foot seven inches. On the rim and border are sculptured two entwined serpents; one of them is feather-headed, the other is not." May we regard them as allusive to the Serpent God and the Serpent Goddess of the Aztec mythology? Mr. Stephens is disposed to regard the singular structure here described as a Gymnasium or Tennis Court, and supports his opinion by a quotation from Herrara. It seems to others much more probable that, with the other buildings of the group, this had an exclusively sacred origin. However that may be, the entwined serpents are clearly symbolical, inasmuch as we find them elsewhere, in a much more conspicuous position, and occupying the first place among the emblematic figures sculptured on the aboriginal temples.

Immediately in connection with this singular structure and constituting part of the eastern wall, is a building, in many respects the most interesting visited by Mr. Stephens, and respecting which it is to be regretted he has not given us a more complete account. It requires no extraordinary effort of fancy to discover in the sculptures and paintings with which it is decorated the pictured records of the teachings of the deified Ku Kulcan, who instructed men in the arts, taught them in religion, and instituted government. There are represented processions of figures, covered with ornaments, and carrying arms. "One of the inner chambers is covered," says Mr. Stephens, "from the floor to the arched roof, with designs in painting, representing, in bright and vivid colours, human figures, battles, horses, boats, trees, and various scenes in domestic life." These correspond very nearly with the representations on the walls of the ancient Buddhist temples of Java, which are described by Mr. Crawford as being covered with designs of "a great variety of subjects, such as processions, audiences, religious worship, battles, hunting, maritime, and other scenes."

Among the ruins of Uxmal is a structure closely resembling the Egclesia of Chichen. It consists of two massive walls of stone, one hundred and twenty-eight feet long, and thirty in thickness, and placed seventy feet apart. So far as could be made out, they are exactly alike in plan and ornament. The sides facing each other are embellished with sculpture, and upon both remain the fragments of entwined colossal serpents which run the whole length of the walls. In the centre of each facade, as at Chichen, were the fragments of a great stone ring, which had been broken off and probably destroyed. It would therefore seem that the emblem of the entwined serpents was significant of the purposes to which these structures were dedicated. The destruction of these stones is another evidence of their religious character; for the conquerors always directed their destroying zeal against those monuments, or parts of monuments, most venerated and valued by the Indians, and which were deemed most intimately connected with their superstitions.

Two hundred feet to the south of this edifice is another large and imposing structure, called Casa de las Monjas, House of the Nuns. It stands on the highest terraces, and is reached by a flight of steps. It is quadrangular in form, with a courtyard in the centre. This is two hundred and fourteen by two hundred and fifty-eight. "Passing through the arched gateway," says Mr. Stephens, "we enter this noble courtyard, with four great facades looking down upon it, each ornamented from one end to the other with the richest and most elaborate carving known in the art of the builders. The facade on the left is most richly ornamented, but is much ruined. It is one hundred and sixty feet long, and is distinguished by two colossal serpents entwined, running through and encompassing nearly all the ornaments is most entire, the tail of one serpent is held up nearly over the head of the other, and has an ornament upon it like a turban with a plume of feathers. There are marks upon the extremity of the tail, probably intended to represent the rattlesnake, with which the country abounds. The lower serpent has its monstrous jaws wide open, and within there is a human head, the face of which is distinctly visible in the stone. The head and tail of the two serpents at the south end of the facade are said to have corresponded with those at the north, and when the whole was entire, in 1836, the serpents were seen encircling every ornament of the building. The bodies of the serpents are covered with feathers. Its ruins present a lively idea of the large and many well-constructed buildings of lime and stone, which Bernal Diaz saw at Campeachy, with figures of serpents and idols painted on their walls." Mr. Norman mentions that the heads of the serpents were adorned with plumes of feathers, and that the tails showed the peculiarity of the rattlesnake. [2]

The eastern facade, opposite that just described, is less elaborately, but more tastefully ornamented. Over each doorway is an ornament representing the Sun. In every instance there is a face in the centre, with the tongue projected, surmounted by an elaborate head-dress; between the bars there is also a range of many lozenge-shaped ornaments, in which the remains of red paint are distinctly visible, and at each end is a serpent's head with the mouth open. The ornament over the principal doorway is much more complicated and elaborate, and of that marked and peculiar style which characterizes the highest efforts of the builders.

The central figure, with the projecting tongue, is probably that of the Sun, and in general design coincides with the central

---

[2] Trav. in Yucatan.

figure sculptured on the great calendar stone of Mexico, and with that found by Mr. Stephens on the walls of Casa No. 3 at Palenque, where it is represented as an object of admiration. The protrusion of the tongue signified, among the Aztecs, ability to speak, and denoted life or existence. Among the Sclavonian nations, the idea of vitality was conveyed by ability to eat, as it is by to breathe among ourselves, and to walk among the Indians of the Algonquin stock.

Although Central America was occupied by nations independent of those of Mexico proper, yet some of them (as those inhabiting the Pacific coast, as far south as Nicaragua) were descended directly from them, and all had striking features in common with them. Their languages were in general different, but cognate; their architecture was essentially the same; and their religion, we have every reason for believing, was not widely different, though doubtless that of the south was less ferocious in its character, and not so generally disfigured by human sacrifices.

We may therefore look with entire safety for common mythological notions, especially when we are assured of the fact that, whatever its modifications, the religion of the continent is essentially the same; and especially when we know that whatever differences may have existed amongst the various nations of Mexico and Central America, the elements of their religion were derived from a common Tottecan root.

CHAPTER VI

The monuments of Mexico representing the serpent are very numerous, and have been specially remarked by nearly every traveller in that interesting country. The symbol is equally conspicuous in the ancient paintings.

"The great temple of Mexico," says Acosta, "was built of great stones in fashion of snakes tied one to another, and the circuit was called coate-pantli which is circuit of snakes." Duran informs us that this temple was expressly built by the first Montezuma "for all the gods," and hence called Coatlan, literally "serpent place." It contained, he also informed us, the temple or shrine of Tezcatlipoca, Huitzlipochtli, and Tlaloc, called Coateocalli, "Temple of the Serpent."

Says Bernal Diaz, in his account of the march of Cortes to Mexico, "We today arrived at a place called Terraguco, which we called the town of the serpents, on account of the enormous figures of those reptiles which we found in their temples, and which they worshipped as gods."

It cannot be supposed that absolute serpent worship---a simple degraded adoration of the reptile itself, or Fetishism, such as is said to exist in some parts of Africa---prevailed in Mexico. The serpent entered into their religious systems only as an emblem. It is nevertheless not impossible, on the contrary it is extremely probable, that a degree of superstitious veneration attached to the reptile itself. According to Bernal Diaz, living rattlesnakes were kept in the great temple of Mexico as sacred objects. He says, "Moreover, in that accursed house they kept vipers and venomous snakes, who had something at their tails which sounded like morris-bells, and these are the worst of vipers. They were kept in cradles and barrels, and in earthen vessels, upon feathers, and there they laid their eggs, and nursed up their snakelings, and they were fed with the bodies of the sacrificed, and with dogs' meat."

Charlevaix in the History of Paraguay, relates "that Alvarez, in one of his expeditions into that country, found a town in which was a large tower or temple the residence of a monstrous serpent which the inhabitants had chosen for a divinity and which they fed with human flesh. He was as thick as an ox, and seven and twenty feet long." This account has been regarded as somewhat apocryphal, although it is likely enough that Serpent Worship may have existed among some of the savage tribes of South America.

It has been said "it should be remarked that Diaz was little disposed to look with complacency upon the religion of the Mexicans, or whatever was connected with it, and that his prejudices were not without their influence on his language. His relation, nevertheless, may be regarded as essentially reliable."

Mr. Mayer, in his Description of Mexico, gives an interesting account of the ancient and extraordinary Indian Pyramid of Cholula, an erection intimately connected with the Quetzalcoatl we have been speaking of.

This is one of the most remarkable relics of the aborigines on the continent, for, although it was constructed only of the adobes or common sun-dried brick, it still remains in sufficient distinctness to strike every observer with wonder at the enterprise of its Indian builders. What it was intended for, whether tomb or temple, no one has determined with certainty, though the wisest antiquarians have been guessing since the conquest. In the midst of a plain the Indians erected a mountain. The base still remains to give us its dimensions; but what was its original height? Was it the tomb of some mighty lord, or sovereign prince; or was it alone a place of sacrifice?

Many years ago in cutting a new road toward Puebla from Mexico it became necessary to cross a portion of the base of this pyramid. The excavation laid bare a square chamber, built of stone, the roof of which was sustained by cypress beams. In it were found some idols of basalt, a number of painted vases, and the remains of two dead bodies. No care was taken of these relics by the discoverers, and they are lost to us for ever.

Approaching the pyramid from the east, it appears so broken and overgrown with trees that it is difficult to make out any outline distinctly. From the west, however, a very fair idea may be obtained of this massive monument as it rises in solitary grandeur from the midst of the wide-spreading plain. A well-paved road cut by the old Spaniards, ascends from the north-west corner with steps at regular intervals, obliquing first on the west side to the upper bench of the terrace, and thence returning toward the same side until it is met by a steep flight rising to the front of the small dome-crowned chapel, surrounded with its grave of cypress and dedicated to the Virgin of Remedies.

The summit is perfectly level, and protected by a parapet wall, whence a magnificent view extends on every side over the level valley. Whatever this edifice may have been, the idea of thus attaining permanently an elevation to which the people might resort for prayer---or even for parade or amusement---was a sublime conception and entitles the men who, centuries ago, patiently erected the lofty pyramid, to the respect of posterity.

There remain at present but four stories of the Pyramid of Cholula, rising above each other and connected by terraces. These stones are formed, as already said, of sun-dried bricks, interspersed with occasional layers of plaster and stone work. "And this is all," says Mr. Mayer, "that is to be told or described. Old as it is---interesting as it is---examined as it has been by antiquaries of all countries---the result has ever been the same. The Indians tell you that it was a place of sepulture, and the Mexicans give you the universal reply of ignorance in this country: Quien Sabe?---who knows? who can tell?"

Baron Humboldt says:---"The Pyramid of Cholula is exactly the same height as that of Tonatiuh Ylxaqual, at Teotihuacan. It is three metres higher than that of Mycerinus, or the third of the great Egyptian pyramids of the group of Djizeh. Its base, however, is larger than that of any pyramid hitherto discovered by travellers in the old world, and is double of that known as the Pyramid of Cheops. Those who wish to form an idea of the immense mass of this Mexican monument by the comparison of objects best known to them, may imagine a square four times greater than that of the Place Vendôme in Paris, covered with layers of bricks rising to twice the elevation of the Louvre. Some persons imagine that the whole of the edifice is not artificial, but as far as explorations have been made there is no reason to doubt that it is entirely a work of art. In its present state (and we are ignorant of its perfect original height) its perpendicular proportion is to its base as eight to one, while in the three great pyramids of Djizeh the proportion is found to be one and six-tenths to one and seven-tenths to one; or nearly as eight to five."

May not this have been the base of some mighty temple destroyed long before the conquest, and of which even the tradition no longer lingers among the neighbouring Indians?

In continuation Humboldt observes "that the inhabitants of Anahuac apparently designed giving the Pyramid of Cholula the same height, and double the base of the Pyramid of Teotihuacan, and that the Pyramid of Asychis, the largest known of the Egyptian, has a base of 800 feet, and is like that of Cholula built of brick. The cathedral of Strasburg is eight feet, and the cross of St. Peter's at Rome forty-one feet lower than the top of the Pyramid of Cheops. Pyramids exist throughout Mexico; in the forests of Papantla at a short distance above the level of the sea; on the plains of Cholula and of Teotihuacan, at the elevations which exceed those of the passes of the Alps. In the most widely distant nations, in climates the most different, man seems to have adopted the same style of construction, the same ornaments, the same customs, and to have placed himself under the government of the same political institutions."

Is this an argument? it has been asked; that all men have sprung from one stock, or that the human mind is the same everywhere, and, affected by similar interests or necessities, invariably comes to the same result, whether pointing a pyramid or an arrow, in making a law or a ladle?

"Much as I distrust," says Mayer, "all the dark and groping efforts of antiquarians, I will nevertheless offer you some sketches and legends which may serve at least to base a conjecture upon as to the divinity to whom this pyramid was erected, and to prove, perhaps, that it was intended as the foundation of a temple and not the covering of a tomb."

A tradition, which has been recorded by a Dominican monk who visited Cholula in 1566, is thus related from his work, by the traveller already quoted.

"Before the great inundation which took place 4,800 years after the erection of the world, the country of Anahuac was inhabited by giants, all of whom either perished in the inundation or were transformed into fishes, save seven who fled into caverns.

"When the waters subsided, one of the giants, called Xelhua, surnamed the 'Architect,' went to Cholula, where as a memorial of the Tlaloc which had served for an asylum to himself and his six brethren, he built an artificial hill in the form of a pyramid. He ordered bricks to be made in the province of Tlalmanalco, at the foot of the Sierra of Cecotl, and in order to convey them to Cholula he placed a file of men who passed them from hand to hand. The gods beheld, with wrath, an edifice the top of which was to reach the clouds. Irritated at the daring attempt of Xelhua, they hurled fire on the pyramid. Numbers of the workmen perished. The work was discontinued, and the monument was afterwards dedicated to Quetzalcoatl." Of this god we have already given a description in these pages.

The following singular story in relation to this divinity and certain services of his temple, is to be found in the "Natural and Moral History of Acosta," book 5, chap. 30.

"There was at this temple of Quetzalcoatl, at Cholula, a court of reasonable greatness, in which they made great dances and pastimes with games and comedies, on the festival day of this idol, for which purpose there was in the midst of this court a theatre of thirty feet square, very finely decked and trimmed----the which they decked with flowers that day---with all the art and invention that might be, being environed around with arches of divers flowers and feathers, and in some places there were tied many small birds, conies, and other tame beasts. After dinner, all the people assembled in this place, and the players presented themselves and played comedies. Some counterfeited the deaf and rheumatic, others the lame, some the blind and crippled which came to seek for cure from the idol. The deaf answered confusedly, the rheumatic coughed, the lame halted, telling their miseries and griefs, wherewith they made the people to laugh. Others came forth in the form of little beasts, some attired like snails, others like toads, and some like lizards; then meeting together they told their offices, and, everyone retiring to his place they sounded on small flutes which was pleasant to hear. They likewise counterfeited butterflies and small birds of divers colours which were represented by the children who were sent to the temple for education. Then they went into a little forest, planted there for the purpose, whence the priests of the temple drew them forth with instruments of music. In the meantime they used many pleasant speeches, some in propounding, others in defending, wherewith the assistants were pleasantly entertained. This done, they made a masque or mummery with all the personages, and so the feast ended."

From these traditions we derive special important facts that Quetzalcoatl was "god of the air;" second, that he was represented as a "feathered serpent;" third, that he was the great divinity of the Cholulans; and fourth, that a hill was raised by them upon which they erected a temple to his glory where they celebrated his festivals with pomp and splendour.

Combining all these, is it unreasonable to believe that the Pyramids of Cholula was the base of this temple, and that he was there worshipped as the Great Spirit of the Air---or of the seasons; the God who produced the fruitfulness of the earth, regulated the Sun, the wind, and the shower, and thus spread plenty over the land. It has been thought too, that the serpent might not improbably typify lightning, and the feathers swiftness, thus denoting one of the attributes of the air---and that the most speedy and destructive.

Mr. Mayer says:---"I constantly saw serpents, in the city of Mexico, carved in stone, and in the various collections of antiquities," and he gives drawings of several of the principal, notably one carved with exquisite skill and found in the courtyard of the University.

Vasquez Coronado, Governor of New Gallicia, as the northern territories of Spain were then called, wrote to the Viceroy Mendoza in 1539, concerning the unknown regions still beyond him to the northward. His account was chiefly based upon the fabulous relation of the Friar Marco Niza, and is not entirely to be relied upon. In this letter he mentions that "in the province of Topira there were people who had great towers and temples covered with straw, with small round windows, filled with human skulls, and before the temple a great round ditch, the brim of which was compassed with a serpent, made of various metals, which held its tail in its mouth, and before which men were sacrificed."

Du Paix has given many examples of the carving representing the snake, which he found in his Antiquarian Explorations in Mexico. One found near the ancient city of Chochimilco represents a snake artificially coiled carved from a block of porphry. "Its long body is gracefully entwined, leaving its head and tail free. There is something showy in the execution of the figure. Its head is elevated and curiously ornamented, its open mouth exhibits two long and pointed fangs, its tongue (which is unusually long) is cloven at the extremity like an anchor, its body is fancifully scaled, and its tail (covered with circles) ends with three rattles. The snake was a frequent emblem with the Mexican artists. The flexibility of its figure rendering it susceptible of an infinite diversity of position, regular and irregular; they availed themselves of this advantage and varied their representations of it without limit and without ever giving it an unnatural attitude."

Near Quauhquechúla, Du Paix found another remarkable sculpture of the serpent carved in black basalt, and so entwined that the space within the folds of its body formed a font sufficiently large to contain a considerable quantity of water. The body of the reptile was spirally entwined, and the head probably served as a handle to move it. It was decorated with circles, and the tail was that of a rattlesnake.

Du Paix also found at Tepeyaca, in a quarter of the town called St. Michael Tlaixegui (signifying in the Mexican language the cavity of the mountain) a serpent carved in red porphry. It is of large dimensions, in an attitude of repose, and coiled upon itself in spiral circles so as to leave a hollow space or transverse axis in the middle. The head, which has a fierce expression, is armed with two long and sharp fangs, and the tongue which has a fierce expression, is armed with two long and sharp fangs, and the tongue is double being divided longitudinally. The entire surface of the body is ornamented or covered with broad and long feathers, and the tail terminates in four rattles. Its length from the head to the extremity of the tail is about twenty feet, and it gradually diminishes in thickness. "This reptile," Du Paix says, "was the monarch or giant of its species, and in pagan times was a deity greatly esteemed under the name Quetzalcoatl, or Feathered Serpent. It is extremely well sculptured, and there are still marks of its having been once painted with vermillion."

But the symbolical feathered serpent was not peculiar to Mexico and Yucatan. Squier, in his Exploration of Nicaragua, several times encountered it. Near the city of Santiago de Managua, the capital of the Republic, situated upon the shores of Lake Managua or Leon, and near the top of the high volcanic ridge which separates the waters flowing into the Atlantic from those running into the Pacific, is an extinct crater, now partially filled with water, forming a lake nearly two miles in circumference, called Nihapa. The sides of this crater are perpendicular rocks ranging from five hundred to eight hundred feet in height. There is but one point where descent is possible. It leads to a little space, formed by the fallen rocks and debris which permits a foothold for the traveller. Standing here, he sees above him, on the smooth face of the cliff, a variety of figures, executed by the aborigines, in red paint. Most conspicuous amongst them, is a feathered serpent coiled and ornamented. It is about four feet in diameter. Upon some of the other rocks were formed paintings of the serpent, perfectly corresponding with the representations in the Dresden MS. copied by Kingsborough and confirming the conjectures of

Humboldt and other investigators that this MS. had its origin to the southward of Mexico. The figure copied was supposed by the natives who had visited it to represent the sun. Some years ago, large figures of the sun and moon were visible upon the cliffs, but the section upon which they were painted was thrown down by the great earthquake of 1838. Parts of the figures can yet be traced upon the fallen fragments.

It is a singular fact that many of the North American Indian tribes entertain a superstitious regard for serpents, and particularly for the rattlesnake. Though always avoiding, they never destroyed it, "lest," says Bartram, "the spirit of the reptile should excite its kindred to revenge."

According to Adair, this fear was not unmingled with veneration. Charlevoix states that the Natchez had the figure of a rattlesnake, carved from wood, placed among other objects upon the altar of their temple, to which they paid great honours. Heckwelder relates that the Linni Linape, called the rattlesnake "grandfather" and would on no account allow it to be destroyed. Henney states that the Indians around Lake Huron had a similar superstition, and also designated the rattlesnake as their "grandfather." He also mentions instances in which offerings of tobacco were made to it, and its parental care solicited for the party performing the sacrifice. Carver also mentions an instance of similar regard on the part of a Menominee Indian, who carried a rattlesnake constantly with him, "treating it as a deity, and calling it his great father."

A portion of the veneration with which the reptile was regarded in these cases may be referred to that superstition so common among the savage tribes, under the influence of which everything remarkable in nature was regarded as a medicine or mystery, and therefore entitled to respect. Still there appears to be, linked beneath all, the remnant of an Ophite superstition of a different character which is shown in the general use of the serpent as a symbol of incorporeal powers, of "Manitous" or spirits.

Mr. James, in his MSS. in the possession of the New York Historical Society, states, "that the Menominees translate the manitou of the Chippeways by ahwahtoke," which means emphatically a snake. "Whether," he continues, "the word was first formed as a name for a surprising or disgusting object, and thence transferred to spiritual beings, or whether the extension of its signification has been in an opposite direction, it is difficult to determine." Bossu also affirms that the Arkansas believed in the existence of a great spirit, which they adore under form of a serpent. In the Northwest it was a symbol of evil power.

Here we may suitably introduce the tradition of a great serpent, which is to this day current amongst a large portion of the Indians of the Algonquin stock. It affords some curious parallelisms with the allegorical relations of the old world. The Great Teacher of the Algonquins, Manabozho, is always placed in antagonism to a great serpent, a spirit of evil, who corresponds very nearly with the Egyptian Typhon, the Indian Kaliya, and the Scandinavian Midgard. He is also connected with the Algonquin notions of a deluge; and as Typhon is placed in opposition to Osiris or Apollo, Kaliya to Surya or the Sun, and Midgard to Wodin or Odin, so does he bear a corresponding relation to Manabozho. The conflicts between the two are frequent; and although the struggles are sometimes long and doubtful, Manabozho is usually successful against his adversary. One of these contests involved the destruction of the earth by water, and its reproduction by the powerful and beneficent Manabozho. The tradition in which this grand event is embodied was thus related by Kah-ge-ga-gah-boowh, a chief of the Ojibway. In all of its essentials, it is recorded by means of the rude pictured signs of the Indians, and scattered all over the Algonquin territories.

One day returning to his lodge, from a long journey, Manabozho missed from it his young cousin, who resided with him, he called his name aloud, but received no answer. He looked around on the sand for the tracks of his feet, and he there, for the first time, discovered the trail of Meshekenabek, the serpent. He then knew that his cousin had been seized by his great enemy. He armed himself, and followed on his track, he passed the great river, and crossed mountains and valleys to the shores of the deep and gloomy lake now called Manitou Lake, Spirit Lake, or the Lake of Devils. The trail of Meshekenabek led to the edge of the water.

At the bottom of this lake was the dwelling of the serpent, and it was filled with evil spirits---his attendants and companions. Their forms were monstrous and terrible, but most, like their master, bore the semblance of serpents. In the centre of this horrible assemblage was Meshekenabek himself, coiling his volumes around the hapless cousin of Manabozho. His head was red as with blood, and his eyes were fierce and glowed like fire. His body was all over armed with hard and glistening scales of every shade and colour.

Manabozho looked down upon the writhing spirits of evil, and he vowed deep revenge. He directed the clouds to disappear from the heavens, the winds to be still, and the air to become stagnant over the lake of the manitous, and bade the sun shine upon it with all its fierceness; for thus he sought to drive his enemy forth to seek the cool shadows of the trees, that grew upon its banks, so that he might be able to take vengeance upon him.

Meanwhile, Manabozho seized his bow and arrows and placed himself near the spot where he deemed the serpent would come to enjoy the shade. He then transferred himself into the broken stump of a withered tree, so that his enemies might not discover his presence.

The winds became still, and the sun shone hot on the lake of the evil manitous. By and by the waters became troubled, and bubbles rose to the surface, for the rays of the sun penetrated to the horrible brood within its depths. The commotion increased, and a serpent lifted its head high above the centre of the lake and gazed around the shores. Directly another came to the surface, and they listened for the footsteps of Manabozho but they heard him nowhere on the face of the earth, and they said one to the other, "Manabozho sleeps." And then they plunged again beneath the waters, which seemed to hiss as they closed over them.

It was not long before the lake of manitous became more troubled than before, it boiled from its very depths, and the hot waves dashed wildly against the rocks on its shores. The commotion increased, and soon Meshekenabek, the Great Serpent, emerged slowly to the surface, and moved towards the shore. His blood-red crest glowed with a deeper hue, and the reflection from his glancing scales was like the blinding glitter of a sleet covered forest beneath the morning sun of winter. He was followed by the evil spirits, so great a number that they covered the shores of the lake with their foul trailing carcases.

They saw the broken, blasted stump into which Manabozho had transformed himself, and suspecting it might be one of his disguises, for they knew his cunning, one of them approached, and wound his tail around it, and sought to drag it down. But Manabozho stood firm, though he could hardly refrain from crying aloud, for the tail of the monster tickled his sides.

The Great Serpent wound his vast folds among the trees of the forest, and the rest also sought the shade, while one was left to listen for the steps of Manabozho.

When they all slept, Manabozho silently drew an arrow from his quiver, he placed it in his bow, and aimed it where he saw the heart beat against the sides of the Great Serpent. He launched it, and with a howl that shook the mountains and startled the wild beasts in their caves, the monster awoke, and, followed by its frightful companions, uttering mingled sounds of rage and terror, plunged again into the lake. Here they vented their fury on the helpless cousin of Manabozho, whose body they tore into a thousand fragments, his mangled lungs rose to the surface, and covered it with whiteness. And this is the origin of the foam on the water.

When the Great Serpent knew that he was mortally wounded, both he and the evil spirits around him were rendered tenfold more terrible by their great wrath and they rose to overwhelm Manabozho. The water of the lake swelled upwards from its dark depths, and with a sound like many thunders, it rolled madly on its track, bearing the rocks and trees before it with resistless fury. High on the crest of the foremost wave, black as the midnight, rode the writhing form of the wounded Meshekenabek, and red eyes glazed around him, and the hot breaths of the monstrous brood hissed fiercely above the retreating Manabozho. Then thought Manabozho of his Indian children, and he ran by their villages, and in a voice of alarm bade them flee to the mountains, for the Great Serpent was deluging the earth in his expiring wrath, sparing no living thing. The Indians caught up their children, and wildly sought safety where he bade them. But Manabozho continued his flight along the base of the western hills, and finally took refuge on a high mountain beyond Lake Superior, for towards the north. There he found many men and animals who had fled from the flood that already covered the valleys and plains, and even the highest hills. Still the waters continued to rise, and soon all the mountains were overwhelmed save that on which stood Manabozho. Then he gathered together timber, and made a raft, upon which the men and women, and the animals that were with him, all placed themselves. No sooner had they done so, than the rising floods closed over the mountain and they floated alone on the surface of the waters; and thus they floated for many days, and some died, and the rest became sorrowful, and reproached Manabozho that he did not disperse the waters and renew the earth that they might live. But though he knew that his great enemy was by this time dead, yet could not Manabozho renew the world unless he had some earth in his hands wherewith to begin the work. And this he explained to those that were with him, and he said that were it ever so little, even a few grains of earth, then could he disperse the waters and renew the world. Then the beaver volunteered to go to the bottom of the deep, and get some earth, and they all applauded her design. She plunged in, they waited long, and when she returned she was dead; they opened her hands but there was no earth in them. "Then," said the otter, "will I seek the earth:" and the bold swimmer dived from the raft. The otter was gone still longer than the beaver, but when he returned to the surface he too was dead, and there was no earth in his claws. "Who shall find the earth?" exclaimed all those left on the raft, "now that the beaver and the otter are dead?" and they desponded more than before, repeating, "Who shall find the earth?" "That will I," said the muskrat, and he quickly disappeared between the logs of the raft. The muskrat was gone very long, much longer than the otter, and it was thought he would never return, when he suddenly rose near by, but he was too weak to speak, and he swam slowly towards the raft. He had hardly got upon it when he too died from his great exertion. They opened his little hands and there, clasped closely between the fingers, they found a few grains of fresh earth. These Manabozho carefully collected and dried them in the sun, and then he rubbed them into a fine powder in his palms, and, rising up, he blew them abroad upon the waters. No sooner was this done than the flood began to subside, and soon the trees on the mountains and hills emerged from the deep, and the plains and the valleys came in view and the waters disappeared from the land leaving no trace but a thick sediment, which was the dust that Manabozho had blow abroad from the raft.

Then it was found that Meshekenabek, the Great Serpent, was dead, and that the evil manitous, his companions, had returned to the depths of the lake of spirits, from which, for the fear of Manabozho, they never more dared to come forth. And in gratitude to the beaver, the otter, and the muskrat, those animals were ever after held sacred by the Indians, and they became their brethren, and they never killed nor molested them until the medicine of the stranger made them forget their relations and turned their hearts to ingratitude.

In the mounds of the West have been found various sculptures of the serpent, and amongst them one as follows:---It represents a coiled rattlesnake, and is carved in a very compact cinnamon-coloured sandstone. It is six and a quarter inches long, one and three-eighths broad, and a quarter of an inch thick. The workmanship is delicate, and the characteristic features of the rattlesnake are perfectly represented; the head, unfortunately, is not entire, but enough remains to show that it was surmounted by some kind of feather-work resembling that so conspicuously represented in the sculptured monuments of the South. It was found carefully enveloped in sheet copper, and under circumstances which render it certain that it was an object of high regard and probably of worship.

Notwithstanding the striking resemblances which have been pointed out, in the elementary religions of the old and new worlds, and the not less remarkable coincidences in their symbolical systems, we are scarcely prepared to find in America that specific combination which fills so conspicuous a place in the early cosmogonies and mythologies of the East, and which constitute the basis of these investigations, namely, the compound symbol of the Serpent and the Egg. It must be admitted that, in the few meagre and imperfect accounts which we have of the notions of cosmogony entertained by the American nations, we have no distinct allusion to it. The symbolism is far too refined and abstract to be adopted by wandering, savage tribes, and we can only look for it, if at all, among the more civilized nations of the central part of the continent, where religion and mythology ranked as an intelligible system. And here we have at once to regret and reprobate the worse than barbarous zeal of the Spanish conquerors, who, not content with destroying the pictured records and over-turning and defacing the primitive monuments of those remarkable nations; distorted the few traditions which they recorded, so as to lend a seeming support to the fictions of their own religion, and invested the sacred rites of the aborigines with horrible and repulsive features, so as to furnish, among people like minded with themselves, some apology for their savage cruelty. Not only were orders given by the first Bishop of Mexico, the infamous Zumanaga, for the burning of all the Mexican MSS. which could be procured, but all persons were discouraged from recording the traditions of the ancient inhabitants.

So far, therefore, from having a complete and consistent account of the beliefs and conceptions of those nations, to which reference may be had in inquiries of this kind, we have only detached and scattered fragments, rescued by later hands from the general destruction. Under such circumstances we cannot expect to find parallel evidences of the existence of specific conceptions; that is to say, we may find certain representations clearly symbolical and referring to the cosmogony, mythology, or religion of the primitive inhabitants and yet look in vain among the scanty and distorted traditions and few mutilated pictured records which are left us for collateral support of the significance which reason and analogy may assign to them.

It is not assumed to say that any distinct representation of the Serpent and the Egg exists amongst the monuments of Mexico or Central America; what future investigations may disclose remains to be seen. If, until the present time, we have remained in profound ignorance of the existence of the grand monument under notice, in one of the best populated states, what treasures of antiquity may yet be hidden in the fastnesses of the central part of the continent!

It has often been said that every feature in the religion of the New World, discovered by Cortez and Pizarro, indicates an origin common to the superstitions of Egypt and Asia. The same solar worship, the same pyramidal monuments, and the same Ophiolatreia distinguish them all.

Acosta says "the temple of Vitziliputzli was built of great stones in fashion of snakes tied one to another, and the circuit was called 'the circuit of snakes' because the walls of the enclosure were covered with the figures of snakes. Vitziliputzli held in his right hand a staff cut in the form of a serpent, and the four corners of the ark in which he was seated terminated each with a carved representation of the head of a serpent. The Mexican century was represented by a circle, having the sun in the centre, surrounded by the symbols of the years. The circumference was a serpent twisted into four knots at the cardinal points."

The Mexican month was divided into twenty days; the serpent and dragon symbolized two of them. In Mexico there was also a temple dedicated to the God of the Air, and the door of it was formed so as to resemble a serpent's mouth. [3]

Amongst other things, Peter Martyr mentions a large serpent-idol at Campeachy, made of stones and bitumen, in the act of devouring a marble lion. When first seen by the Spaniards it was warm with the blood of human victims.

"Ancient painting and sculptures abound with evidences of Mexican Ophiolatreia, and prove that there was scarcely a Mexican deity who was not symbolized by a serpent or a dragon. Many deities appear holding serpents in their hands, and small figures of priests are represented with a snake over each head. This reminds us forcibly of the priests of the Egyptian Isis, who are described in sculpture with the sacred asp upon the head and a cone in the left hand. And to confirm the original mutual connexion of all the serpent-worshippers throughout all the world---the Mexican paintings, as well as the Egyptian and Persian hieroglyphics, describe the Ophite Hierogram of the intertwined serpents in almost all its varieties. A very remarkable one occurs in M. Allard's collection of sculptures; in which the dragons forming it have each a man's head in his mouth. The gods of Mexico are frequently pictured fighting with serpents and dragons; and gods, and sometimes men, are represented in conversation with the loathsome creatures. There is scarcely, indeed, a feature in the mystery of Ophiolatreia which may not be recognised in the Mexican superstitions.

We perceive, therefore, that in the kingdom of Mexico the serpent was sacred, and emblematic of more gods than one: an observation which may be extended to almost every other nation which adored the symbolical serpent. This is a remarkable and valuable fact, and it discovers in Ophiolatreia another feature of its aboriginal character. For it proves the serpent to have been a symbol of intrinsic divinity, and not a mere representative of peculiar properties which belong to some gods and not to others." [4]

---

[3] Faber
[4] Deane.

From what has been presented, it will be seen that the serpent symbol was of general acceptance in America, particularly among the semi-civilised nations; that it entered widely into their symbolic representations, and this significance was essentially the same with that which attached to it among the early nations of the old continent. Upon the basis, therefore, of the identity which we have observed in the elementary religious conceptions of the Old and New World, and the striking uniformity in their symbolical systems, we feel justified in ascribing to the emblematic Serpent and Egg of Ohio a significance radically the same with that which was assigned to the analogous compound symbol among the primitive nations of the East. This conclusion is further sustained by the character of some of the religious structures of the old continent, in which we find the symbolic serpent and the egg or circle represented on a most gigantic scale. Analogy could probably furnish no more decisive sanction, unless by exhibiting other structures, in which not only a general correspondence, but an absolute identity should exist. Such an identity it would be unreasonable to look for, even in the works of the same people, constructed in accordance with a common design.

It may seem hardly consistent with the caution which should characterize researches of this kind, to hazard the suggestion that the symbolical Serpent and Egg of Ohio are distinctly allusive to the specific notions of cosmogony which prevailed among the nations of the East, for the reason that it is impossible to bring positive collateral proof that such notions were entertained by any of the American nations. The absence of written records and of impartially preserved traditions we have already had ample reason to deplore; and unless further explorations shall present us with unexpected results, the deficiency may always exist. But we must remember that in no respect are men more tenacious than in the preservation of their rudimental religous beliefs and early conceptions. In the words of a philosophical investigator---"Of all researches that most effectually aid us to discover the origin of a nation or people whose history is involved in the obscurity of ancient times, none perhaps are attended with such important results as the analysis of their theological dogmas and their religious practices. To such matters mankind adhere with the greatest tenacity, which, though modified and corrupted in the revolution of ages, still retain features of their original construction, when language, arts, sciences and political establishments no longer preserve distinct lineaments of their ancient constitutions." [5]

A striking example of the truth of these remarks is furnished in the religion of India, which, to this day, notwithstanding the revolution of time and empire, the destruction of foreign and of civil wars, and the constant addition of allegorical fictions (more fatal to the primitive system than all the other causes combined), still retains its original features, which are easily recognisable, and which identify it with the religions which prevailed in monumental Egypt, on the plains of Assyria, in the valleys of Greece, among the sterner nations around the Caspian, and among their kindred tribes on the rugged shores of Scandinavia.

This tenacity is not less strikingly illustrated in the careful perpetuation of rites, festivals and scenic representations which originated in notions which have long since become obsolete, and are now forgotten. Very few of the attendants on the annual May-day festival, as celebrated a few years back in this country, and very few of those who have read about the same are aware that it was only a perpetuation of the vernal solar festival of Baal, and that the garlanded pole was anciently a Phallic emblem.

---

[5] McCulloch's American Researches, p. 225.

CHAPTER VII.

Egypt, of all ancient nations the most noted for its idolatry, was in its earliest days the home of the peculiar worship we are contemplating. A learned writer on the subject says "the serpent entered into the Egyptian religion under all his characters---of an Emblem of Divinity, a Charm or Oracle, and a God." Cneph, Thoth and Isis were conspicuous and chief among the gods and goddesses thus symbolized, though he is said to have entered more or less into the symbolical worship of all the gods.

Sanchoniathon describes Thoth as the founder of Serpent Worship in Egypt, and he is generally regarded as the planter of the earliest colonies in Phœnicia and Egypt after the Deluge. He has been called the Reformer of the Religions of Egypt, and Deane says: "He taught the Egyptians (or rather that part of his colony which was settled in Egypt) a religion, which, partaking of Zabaism and Ophiolatreia, had some mixture also of primeval truth. The Divine Spirit he denominated Cneph, and described him as the Original, Eternal Spirit, pervading all creation, whose symbol was a serpent."

Cneph was called by the priests the architect of the universe, and has been represented as a serpent with an egg in his mouth; the serpent being his hieroglyphical emblem, and the egg setting forth the mundane elements as proceeding from him.

After his death Thoth was, in return for services rendered to the people, made a god of---the god of health, or of healing, and so became the prototype of Æsculapius. His learning appears to have been great, and he instructed the people in astronomy, morals, hieroglyphics and letters. He is generally represented leaning upon a knotted stick which has around it a serpent.

The mysteries of the worship of Isis abounded in allusions to the serpent, and Montfaucon says that the Isaic table, a plate of brass overlaid with brass enamel; intermixed with plates of silver, which described the mysteries, was charged with serpents in every part as emblems of the goddess. The particular serpent thus employed was that small one well known as the instrument used in her suicide by the celebrated Cleopatra, the asp. This creature is pictured and carved on the priestly robes, the tiaras of the kings, the image of the goddess. The British Museum possesses a head of this divinity wearing a coronet of them. Not only so, the living reptiles were kept in her temple and were supposed to sanctify the offerings by crawling about amongst them.

As we have said the serpent entered largely into the symbolical worship of all the Egyptian deities, and Cneph, Thoth and Isis can only be regarded as three of the chief.

Deane says there is scarcely an Egyptian deity which is not occasionally symbolized by it. Several of these deities are represented with their proper heads terminating in serpents' bodies. In Montfaucon, vol. 2, plate 207, there is an engraving of Serapis with a human head and serpentine tail. Two other minor gods are also represented, the one by a serpent with a bull's head, the other by a serpent with the radiated head of the lion. The second of these, which Montfaucon supposes to be an image of Apis, is bored through the middle: probably with a design to hang about the neck, as they did many other small figures of gods, by way of ornament or charms.

The figure of Serapis encircled by serpents is found on tombs. The appearance of serpents on tombs was very general. On an urn of Egnatius, Nicephoras, and of Herbasia Clymene, engraved in Montfaucon, vol. 5, a young man entwined by a serpent is described as falling headlong to the ground. In the urn of Herbasia Clymene the corners are ornamented with figures of serpents. It is a singular coincidence that the creature by whom it is believed came death into the world should be consecrated by the earliest heathen idolaters to the receptacles of the dead. It is remarkable also that Serapis was supposed by the Egyptians to have dominion over evil demons, or in other words was the same as Plato or Satan."

On some of the Egyptian temples the serpent has been conspicuously figured as an emblem consecrated to the Divine service. Thus it is found at Luxore, Komombu, Dendara, Apollinopolis and Esnay. The Pamphylian obelisk also bears it many times---fifty-two it is said---and according to Pococke each of the pillars of the temple of Gava has it twice sculptured.

All writers on the subject have noticed the variations of form under which the serpent has appeared on Egyptian monuments, and have laid stress upon it as indicating the great consideration in which he was held. There is little to be wondered at in this when we remember that he was regarded as symbolical of divine wisdom, power, and creative energy; of immortality and regeneration, from the shedding of his own skin; and of eternity, when represented in the act of biting his own tail.

One writer says the world was represented by a circle, intersected by two diameters perpendicular to each other, which diameters, according to Eusebius, were serpents. Jablonski says the circumference only, was a serpent.

Kircher says that the elements (or rather what were so considered in ancient times) were represented by serpents. Earth was symbolized by a prostrate two-horned snake; water, by a serpent moving in an undulated manner; air, by an erect serpent in the act of hissing; fire, by an asp standing on its tail and bearing upon his head a globe. "From these hieroglyphics," remarks Deane, "It is clear that the serpent was the most expressive symbol of divinity with the Egyptians."

An engraving in Montfaucon, vol. 2, p. 237, calls for notice here, as illustrating the great extent to which the veneration of the serpent once prevailed in Egypt. In the year 1694, in an old wall of Malta, was discovered a plate of gold, supposed to have been concealed there by its possessors at a time when everything idolatrous was destroyed as abominable. Montfaucon says: "This plate was rolled up in a golden casket; it consists of two long rows which contain a very great number of Egyptian deities, most of which have the head of some beast or bird. Many serpents are also seen intermixed, the arms and legs of the gods terminating in serpents' tails. The first figure has upon its back a long shell with a serpent upon it; in each row there is a serpent extended upon an altar. Among the figures of the sacred row there is seen an Isis of tolerably good form. This same plate, no doubt, contains the most profound mysteries of the Egyptian superstition."

It hardly matters where we look in Egypt, this same serpent symbol is found entering into the composition of everything, whether ornamental, useful, or ecclesiastical. The basilisk, the most venomous of all snakes, and so regarded as the king of the species and named after the oracular god of Canaan OB or OUB, was represented on coins with rays upon his head like a crown; around the coin was inscribed "Agathodæmon." The emperor Nero in the "madness of his vanity," it is said, caused a number of such coins to be struck with the inscription "The New Agathodæmon," meaning himself.

The Egyptians held basilisks in such veneration that they made images of them in gold and consecrated and placed them in the temples of their gods. Bryant thinks that they were the same as the Thermuthis, or deadly asp. These creatures the Egyptians priests are said to have preserved by digging holes for them in the corners of their temples, and it was a part of their superstition to believe that whosoever was accidentally bitten by them was divinely favoured.[6]

Deane further mentions that the serpent is sometimes found sculptured, and attached to the breasts of mummies; but whether with a view to talismanic security, or as indicative of the priesthood of Isis, is doubtful. A female mummy, opened by M. Passalacqua at Paris some years ago, was adorned with a necklace of serpents carved in stone.

Bracelets, in the form of serpents, were worn by the Grecian women in the time of Clemens Alexdrinus, who thus reproves the fashion:---"The women are not ashamed to place about them the most manifold symbols of the evil one; for as the serpent deceived Eve, so the golden trinket in the fashion of a serpent misleads the women." The children also wore chaplets of the same kind.

---

[6] Gesner, Hist. Anim. p. 54, citing Ælian.

We must not omit to notice the Caduceus, which forms, it is said, one of the most striking examples of the talismanic serpent. According to Montfaucon, Kirchen and others, the notion that this belonged exclusively to Hermes or Mercury is erroneous, as it can be seen in the hand of Cybele, Minerva Amebis, Hercules Ogmius and the personified constellation Virgo, said by Lucian to have had her symbol in the Pythian priestess.

Variously represented in the main, the Caduceus always preserved the original design of a winged wand entwined by two serpents. It is found sometimes without the wings, but never without the serpents; the varieties consisting chiefly in the number of folds made by the serpents' bodies round the wand, and the relative positions of the wings and serpents' heads. It was regarded as powerful in paralyzing the mind and raising the dead.

Kirchen says that Caduceus was originally expressed by the simple figure of a cross by which its inventor, Thoth, is said to have symbolized the four elements proceeding from a common centre.

"Ophiolatreia," says Deane, "had taken such deep root in Egypt that the serpent was not merely regarded as an emblem of divinity, but even held in estimation as the instrument of an oracle. The priests of the temple of Isis had a silver image of a serpent so constructed as to enable a person in attendance to move its head without being observed by the supplicating votary.

"But Egyptian superstition was not contented with worshipping divinity through its emblem the serpent. The senseless idolator soon bowed before the symbol itself, and worshipped this reptile, the representative of man's energy, as a god."

In addition to the temple of the great serpent-god Cneph at Elephantina, there was a renowned one of Jupiter at Thebes, where the practice of Ophiolatreia was carried to a great length. Herodotus writes: "At Thebes there are two serpents, by no means injurious to men; small in size, having two horns springing up from the top of the head. They bury these when dead in the temple of Jupiter: for they say that they are sacred to that god."

Ælian says: "In the time of Ptolemy Euergetes, a very large serpent was kept in the temple of Æsculapius at Alexandria, and in another place a live one of great magnitude was kept and adored with divine honours; the name of this place he called Melité." He gives the following story:---"This serpent had priests and ministers, a table and a bowl. The priests every day carried into the sacred chamber a cake made of flour and honey and then retired. Returning the next day they always found the bowl empty. On one occasion, one of the priests, being extremely anxious to see the sacred serpent, went in alone, and having deposited the cake retired. When the serpent had ascended the table to his feast, the priest came in, throwing open the door with great violence: upon which the serpent departed with great indignation. But the priest was shortly after seized with a mental malady, and, having confessed his crime, became dumb and wasted away until he died."

In Hewart's tables of Egyptian hieroglyphics we see a priest offering adoration to a serpent. The same occurs on the Isiac table.

"In a tomb at Biban, at Malook, is a beautiful painting descriptive of the rites of Ophiolatreia. The officiating priest is represented with a sword in his hand, and three headless victims are kneeling before an immense serpent. Isis is seen sitting under the arch made by the serpent's body, and the sacred asp, with a human face, is behind her seated on the serpent's tail. This picture proves that the serpent was propitiated by human victims."

It is noteworthy that in Egypt as in Phœnicia and other places serpent worship was not immediately destroyed by the advance of Christianity. The Gnostics united it with the religion of the cross, and a quotation from Bishop Pococke will, just here, be most appropriate and interesting.

"We came to Raigny, where the religious sheikh of the famous Heredy was at the side of the river to meet us. He went with us to the grotto of the serpent that has been so much talked of under the name of the Sheikh Heredy, of which I shall give you a particular account, in order to show the folly, credulity, and superstition of these people; for the Christians have faith in it as well as the Turks. We went ascending between the rocky mountain for half a mile, and came to a part where the valley opens wider. On the right is a mosque, built with a dome over it, against the side of the rock, like a sheikh's burial-place. In it there is a large cleft in the rock out of which they say the serpent comes. There is a tomb in the mosque, in the Turkish manner, that they say is the tomb of Heredy, which would make one imagine that one of their saints is buried there, and that they suppose his soul may be in the serpent, for I observed that they went and kissed the tomb with much devotion and said their prayers at it. Opposite to this cleft there is another, which they say is the tomb of Ogli Hassan, that is of Hassan, the son of Heredy; there are two other clefts which they say are inhabited by saints or angels. The sheikh told me there were two of these serpents, but the common notion is that there is only one. He said it had been there ever since the time of Mahomet. The shape of it is like that of other serpents of the harmless breed. He comes out only during the four summer months, and it is said that they sacrifice to it. This the sheikh denied, and affirmed they only brought lambs, sheep, and money to buy oil for the lamps---but I saw much blood and entrails of beasts lately killed before the door.

"The stories are so ridiculous that they ought not to be repeated, if it were not to give an instance of their idolatry in those parts in this respect, though the Mahometan religion seems to be very far from it in other things. They say the virtue of this serpent is to cure all diseases of those who go to it.

"They are also full of a story, that when a number of women go there once a year, he passes by and looks on them, and goes and twines about the neck of the most beautiful.

"I was surprised to hear a grave and sensible Christian say that he always cured any distempers, but that worse followed. And some really believe that he works miracles, and say it is the devil mentioned in Tobit, whom the angel Gabriel drove into the utmost parts of Egypt."

CHAPTER VIII

Bryant and Faber both derive the name of "Europe" from "Aur-ab, the solar serpent." "Whether this be correct or not," says Deane, "it is certain that Ophiolatreia prevailed in this quarter of the globe at the earliest period of idolatry. The first inhabitants of Europe are said to have been the offspring of a woman, partly of the human and partly of the dracontic figure, a tradition which alludes to their Ophite origin.

"Of the countries of Europe, Greece was first colonized by Ophites, but at separate times, both from Egypt and Phœnicia; and it is a question of some doubt, though perhaps of little importance, whether the leader of the first colony, the celebrated Cadmus, was a Phœnician or an Egyptian. Bochart has shown that Cadmus was the leader of the Canaanites who fled before the arms of the victorious Joshua; and Bryant has proved that he was an Egyptian, identical with Thoth. But as mere names of individuals are of no importance, when all agree that the same superstition existed contemporaneously in the two countries, and since Thoth is declared by Sanchoniathan to have been the father of the Phœnician as well as Egyptian Ophiolatreia; we may endeavour without presumption to reconcile the opinions of these learned authors by assuming each to be right in his own line of argument."

In Greece there are numerous traces of the worship of the serpent---it was so common indeed at one time that Justin Martyr declared the people introduced it into the mysteries of all their gods. In the mysteries and excesses of Bacchus it is well-known, of course, to have played a conspicuous part. The people bore them entwined upon their heads, and carrying them in their hands, swung them about crying aloud, "enia, enia." The sign of the Bacchic ceremonies was a consecrated serpent, and in the processions a troop of virgins of noble family carried the reptile with golden baskets containing sesamum, honey cakes and grains of salt, articles all specially connected with serpent worship. The first may be seen in the British Museum, in the hands of priests kneeling before the sacred serpent of Egypt. Honey cakes, according to Herodotus, were presented once a month as food to the sacred serpent in the Acropolis at Athens.

The most remarkable feature of all in the Bacchic orgies is said to have been the mystic serpent. "The mystery of religion was throughout the world concealed in a chest or box. As the Israelites had their sacred ark, every nation upon earth had some holy receptacle for sacred things and symbols. The story of Ericthonius is illustrative of this remark. He was the fourth King of Athens, and his body terminated in the tails of serpents, instead of legs. He was placed by Minerva in a basket, which she gave to the daughter of Cecrops, with strict injunctions not to open it. Here we have a fable made out of the simple fact of the mysterious basket, in which the sacred serpent was carried at the orgies of Bacchus. The whole legend relates to Ophiolatreia. In accordance with the general practice, the worshippers of Bacchus carried in their consecrated baskets or chests the Mystery of their God, together with the offerings." [7]

At the banquets of the Bacchantes, or rather, after them, it was usual to carry round a cup, which was called the "cup of the good dæmon." The symbol of this dæmon was a serpent, as seen on the medals of the town of Dionysopolis in Thrace. On one side were the heads of Gordian and Serapis on the other a coiled serpent.

The serpent was mixed up to a considerable extent with the worship of many other of the Grecian deities. The statues, by Phidias, of Minerva, represent her as decorated with this emblem. In ancient medals, as shown by Montfaucon, she sometimes holds a caduceus in her right hand; at other times she has a staff around which a serpent is twisted, and at others, a large serpent appears going in front of her; while she is sometimes seen with her crest composed of a serpent. It is remarkable too, that in the Acropolis

---

[7] Deane.

at Athens was kept a live serpent who was generally considered the guardian of the place, and Athens was a city specially consecrated to Minerva.

Examples of Grecian Ophiolatreia might easily be multiplied to a considerable extent, but we have space for little more than a brief glance. It is known that upon the walls of Athens was a sculptured head of Medusa, whose hair was intertwined with snakes, and in the temple at Tega was a similar figure which was supposed to possess talismanic power to preserve or destroy. The print in Montfaucon represents the face of Medusa as mild and beautiful, but the serpents as threatening and terrible. There is a story current, that a priestess going into a sanctuary of Minerva in the dead of the night, saw a vision of that goddess, who held up her mantle upon which was impressed a Medusa's head, and that the sight of this fearful object instantaneously converted the intruder into stone.

The armour of Agamemnon, king of Argos, was ornamented with a three-headed serpent; Menelaus, king of Sparta, had one on his shield, and the Spartan people, with the Athenians, affirmed they were of serpentine origin and called themselves ophiogenœ.

At Epidaurus, according to Pausanias, live serpents were kept and fed regularly by servants, who, on account of religious awe, were fearful of approaching the sacred reptiles which in themselves were of the most harmless character. The statue of Æsculapius, at this temple, represented him resting one hand upon the head of a serpent, while his sister, Hygeia, had one twisted about her. It is reported that the god Æsculapius was conveyed by a woman named Nicagora, the wife of Echetimus, to Sicyon under the form of a serpent.

Livy, Ovid, Florus, Valerius Maximus, and Aurelius Victor, relate that a pestilence of a violent and fatal character once broke out in Rome, and that the oracle of Delphi advised an embassy to Epidaurus to fetch the god Æsculapius. This advice was taken, and a company of eleven were sent with the humble supplications of the senate and people of Rome. While they were gazing at the statue of the god, a serpent, "venerable, not horrible," say these authors, which rarely appeared but when he intended to confer some extraordinary benefit, glided from his lurking place, and having passed through the city went directly to the Roman vessel and coiled himself up in the berth of Ogulnius the principal ambassador. Setting sail with the god, they duly arrived off Antium, when the serpent leaped into the sea, and swam to the nearest temple of Apollo, and after a few days returned. But when they entered the Tiber, he leaped upon an island, and disappeared. Here the Romans erected a temple to him in the shape of a ship, and the plague was stayed with wonderful celerity.

Delphi appears to have been the principal stronghold of serpent worship in Greece. Strabo says its original name was Pytho---derived from the serpent Python, slain there by Apollo. From this story Heinsius concludes that the god Apollo was first worshipped at Delphi, under the symbol of a serpent. It is known that the public assemblies at Delphi were called Pythis, these were originally intended for the adoration of the Python.

In Gibbon and the Annales Turcici we have interesting matter about the serpentine column. The former says it was taken from Delphi to Constantinople by the founder of the latter city and set up on a pillar in the Hippodrome. Montfaucon, however, thinks that Constantine only caused a similar column to be made, and that the original remained in its place. Deane says, "this celebrated relic of Ophiolatreia is still to be seen in the same place, where it was set up by Constantine, but one of the serpent's heads is mutilated."

From the Annales we get the following explanations of this inquiry. "When Mahomet came to Atmeidan he saw there a stone column, on which was placed a three-headed brazen serpent. Looking at it, he asked, 'What idol is that?' and, at the same time, hurling his iron mace with great force knocked off the lower jaw of one of the serpent's heads. Upon which, immediately, a great number of serpents began to be seen in the city. Whereupon some advised him to leave that serpent alone from henceforth, since through that image it happened that there were no serpents in the city. Wherefore that column remains to this day. And although in consequence of the lower jaw of the brazen serpent being struck off, some serpents do come into the city, yet they do no harm to no one."

Commenting upon this story Deane remarks---"This traditionary legend, preserved by Leunclavius, marks the stronghold which Ophiolatreia must have taken upon the minds of the people of Constantinople, so as to cause this story to be handed down to so late an era as the seventeenth century. Among the Greeks who resorted to Constantinople were many idolaters of the old religion, who would wilfully transmit any legend favourable to their own superstition. Hence, probably, the charm mentioned above, was attached by them to the Delphic serpent on the column in the Hippodrome, and revived (after the partial mutilation of the figure) by their descendants, the common people, who are always the last in every country to forego an ancient superstition. Among the common people of Constantinople, there were always many more Pagans than Christians at heart. With the Christian religion, therefore, which they professed, would be mingled many of the pagan traditions which were attached to the monuments of antiquity that adorned Byzantium, or were imported into Constantinople.

CHAPTER IX

It will probably be a matter of surprise to many, but it is a fact that even in Britain in ancient times Ophiolatreia largely prevailed. Deane says: "Our British ancestors, under the tuition of the venerable Druids, were not only worshippers of the solar deity, symbolized by the serpent, but held the serpent, independent of his relation to the sun, in peculiar veneration. Cut off from all intercourse with the civilized world, partly by their remoteness and partly by their national character, the Britons retained their primitive idolatry long after it yielded in the neighbouring countries to the polytheistic corruptions of Greece and Egypt. In process of time, however, the gods of the Gaulish Druids penetrated into the sacred mythology of the British and furnished personifications for the different attributes of the dracontic god Hu. This deity was called "The Dragon Ruler of the World" and his car was drawn by serpents. His priests in accomadation with the general custom of the Ophite god, were called after him "Adders." [8]

In a poem of Taliessin, translated by Davies, in his Appendix No. 6, is the following enumeration of a Druid's titles:---

"I am a Druid; I am an architect; I am a prophet;

I am a serpent" (Gnadr).

From the word "Gnadr" is derived "adder," the name of a species of snake. Gnadr was probably pronounced like "adder" with a nasal aspirate.

The mythology of the Druids contained also a goddes "Ceridwen," whose car was drawn by serpents. It is conjectured that this was the Grecian "Ceres;" and not without reason, for the interesting intercourse between the British and Gaulish Druids introduced into the purer religion of the former many of the corruptions ingrafted upon that of the latter by the Greeks and

---

[8] Davies' Mythol. of Druids.

Romans. The Druids of Gaul had among them many divinities corresponding with those of Greece and Rome. They worshipped Ogmius (a compound deity between Hercules and Mercury), and after him, Apollo, Mars, Jupiter, and Minerva, or deities resembling them. Of these they made images; whereas hitherto the only image in the British worship was the great wicker idol into which they thrust human victims designed to be burnt as an expiatory sacrifice for the sins of some chieftain.

The following translation of a Bardic poem, descriptive of one of their religious rites, identifies the superstition of the British Druids with the aboriginal Ophiolatreia, as expressed in the mysteries of Isis of Egypt. The poem is entitled "the Elegy of Uther Pendragon;" that is, of Uther, "The Dragon's Head;" and it is not a little remarkable that the word "Draig" in the British language signifies, at the same time, a fiery serpent, a dragon, and the Supreme God." [9]

In the second part of this poem is the following sacrificial rites of Uther Pendragon:----

"With solemn festivity round the two lakes;
With the lake next my side;
With my side moving round the sanctuary;
While the sanctuary is earnestly invoking
The Gliding King, before whom the Fair One
Retreats upon the veil that covers the huge stones;
Whilst the Dragon moves round over
The places which contain vessels
Of drink offering;
Whilst the drink offering is in the Golden Horns;
Whilst the golden horns are in the hand;
Whilst the knife is upon the chief victim,
Sincerely I implore thee, O victorious Bell, etc., etc.,"

This is a most minute and interesting account of the religious rites of the Druids, proving in clear terms their addiction to Ophiolatreia: for we have not only the history of the "Gliding

---

[9] Owen's Dict. Art. Draig.

King," who pursues "The Fair One," depicted upon "the veil which covers the huge stones"---a history which reminds us most forcibly of the events in Paradise, under a poetic garb; but we have, likewise, beneath that veil, within the sacred circle of "the huge stones," the "Great Dragon, a Living Serpent," moving round the places which contain the vessels of drink-offering; or in other words, moving round the altar stone in the same manner as the serpent in the Isiac mysteries passed about the sacred vessels containing the offerings.

The Golden Horns which contained the drink offerings were very probably of the same kind as that found in Tundera, in Denmark.

The sanctity of the serpent showed itself in another very curious part of the superstition of the British Druids, namely, in that which related to the formation and virtues of the celebrated anguinum, as it is called by Pliny, or gleinen nadroeth, that is, "snake-stones," as they were called by the Britons." Sir R. C. Hoare in his Modern Wiltshire, Hundred of Amesbury, gives an engraving of one, and says: "This is a head of imperfect vitrification representing two circular lines of opaque skylight and white, which seem to represent a snake twined round a centre which is perforated." Mr. Lhwyd, the Welsh antiquary, writing to Ralph Thornley says:---"I am fully satsified that they were amulets of the Druids. I have seen one of them that had nine small snakes upon it. There are others that have one or two or more snakes."

A story comes to us, on Roman authority (that of Pliny), that a knight entering a court of justice wearing an anguinum about his neck was ordered by Claudius to be put to death, it being believed that the influence would improperly wrest judgment in his favour.

Of this anguinum (a word derived from anguis, a snake) Pliny says: "An infinite number of snakes, entwined together in the heat of summer, roll themselves into a mass, and from the saliva of their jaws and the froth of their bodies is engendered an egg, which is called 'anguinum.' By the violent hissing of the serpents the egg is forced into the air, and the Druid destined to secure it, must catch it in his sacred vest before it reaches the ground."

Information relative to the prevalence of this superstition in England will be found in Davies' Myths of the Druids, Camden's Britannia, and Borlase's Cornwall.

Perhaps the most remarkable of all British relics of this worship are to be found on the hills overlooking the village of Abury, in the county of Wiltshire. There, twenty-six miles from the celebrated ruins of Stonehenge, are to be found the remains of a great Serpentine Temple---one of the most imposing, as it certinaly is one of the most interesting, monuments of the British Islands. It was first accurately described by Dr. Stukeley in 1793 in his celebrated work entitled Abury, a Temple of the British Druids. It was afterwards carefully examined by Sir R. C. Hoare and an account published in his elaborate work Ancient Wiltshire. Dr. Stukeley was the first to detect the design of the structure and his conclusions have been sustained by the observations of every antiquary who has succeeded him.

The temple of Abury consisted originally of a grand circumvallation of earth 1,400 feet in diameter, enclosing an area of upwards of twenty-two acres. It has an inner ditch and the height of the embankment, measuring from the bottom of the ditch, is seventeen feet. It is quite regular, though not an exact circle in form, and has four entrances at equal distances apart, though nearly at right angles to each other. Within this grand circle were originally two double or concentric circles composed of massive upright stones: a row of large stones, one hundred in number, was placed upon the inner brow of the ditch. Extending upon either hand from this grand central structure were parallel lines of huge upright stones, constituting, upon each side, avenues upwards of a mile in length. These formed the body of the serpent. Each avenue consisted of two hundred stones. The head of the serpent was represented by an oval structure consisting of two concentric lines of upright stones; the outer line containing forty, the inner eighteen stones. This head rests upon an eminence known as Overton, or Hakpen Hill, from which is commanded a view of the entire structure, winding back for more than two miles to the point of the tail, towards Bekhampton.

Hakpen in the old British dialects signifies Hak, serpent, and pen, head, i.e., Head of the Serpent. "To our name of Hakpen," says Stukeley, "alludes ochim, called 'doleful creatures' in our translation." Isa (13 v. 21), speaking of the desolation of Babylon, says: Wild beasts of the desert shall lie there, and their houses shall be full of ochim, and owls shall dwell there, and satyrs shall dance there." St. Jerome translates it "serpents." The Arabians call a serpent Haie, and wood-serpents Hageshin; and thence our Hakpen; Pen is "head" in British.

"That the votaries of Ophiolatreia penetrated into every part of Britain is probable from the vestiges of some such idolatry even now to be found in Scotland and the western isles. Several obelisks remain in the vicinity of Aberdeen, Dundee and Perth, upon which appear devices strongly indicative of Ophiolatreia. They are engraved in Gordon" Itinerarium Septentrionale. The serpent is a frequent and conspicuous hieroglyphic. From the Runic characters traced upon some of these stones it is conjectured that they were erected by the Danes. Such might have been the case; but the Danes themselves were a sect of Ophites, and had not the people of the country been Ophites also, they might not have suffered these monuments to remain." [10]

Remains indicating the presence of Serpent Worship in Ireland are extremely scarce, but we must remember the story prevalent in the country, accepted as truthful by a large majority of its inhabitants, that St. Patrick banished all snakes from Ireland by his prayers. After all, this may mean nothing more than that by his preaching he overturned and uprooted the superstitious practices of the serpent worshippers of his times.

---

[10] Moor's Hindu Pantheon 342.

CHAPTER X

In the course of this work we have had occasion frequently to allude to India as the home of the peculiar worship before us, and perhaps that country may fairly be placed side by side with Egypt for the multitude of illustrations it affords of what we are seeking to elucidate.

Mr. Rivett-Carnac, from whose paper in the journal of the Bengal Asiatic Society we have already quoted, says:---"The palace of the Bhonslahs at Benares brings me to Nágpúr, where, many years ago, I commenced to make, with but small success, some rough notes on Serpent Worship. Looking up some old sketches, I find that the Mahádeo in the oldest temples at Nágpúr is surmounted by the Nág as at Benares. And in the old temple near the palace of the Nágpúr, or city of the Nág or cobra, is a five-headed snake, elaborately coiled. The Bhonslahs apparently took the many-coiled Nág with them to Benares. A similar representation of the Nág is found in the temple near the Itwarah gate at Nágpúr. Here again the Nág or cobra is certainly worshipped at Mahádeo or the phallus, and there are certain obvious points connected with the position assumed by the cobra when excited and the expansion of the hood, which suggest the reason for this snake in particular being adopted as a representation of the phallus and an emblem of Siva.

"The worship of the snake is very common in the old Nágpúr Province where, especially among the lower class, the votaries of Siva or Nág Bhushan, 'he who wears snakes as his ornaments,' are numerous. It is likely enough that the city took its name from the Nág temple, still to be seen there, and that the river Nág, perhaps, took its name from the city or temple, and not the city from the river, as some think. Certain it is that many of the Kunbi or cultivating class worship the snake and the snake only, and that this worship is something more than the ordinary superstitious awe with which all Hindus regard the snake. I find from my notes that one Kunbi whom I questioned in old days, when I was a Settlement Officer in camp in the Nágpúr Division, stated that he worshipped the Nág and nothing else; that he worshipped clay images of the snake, and when he could afford to pay snake-catchers for a look at a live one, he worshipped the living snake; that if he saw a Nág on the road he would worship it, and that he believed no Hindu would kill a Nág or cobra if he knew it were a Nág. He then gave me the following list of articles he would use in worshipping the snake, when he could afford it; and I take it, the list is similar to what would be used in ordinary Siva Worship. 1---Water. 2---Gandh, pigment of sandal-wood for the forehead or body. 3---Cleaned rice. 4---Flowers. 5----Leaves of the Bail tree. 6---Milk. 7---Curds. 8---A thread or piece of cloth. 9---Red powder. 10---Saffron. 11---Abir, a powder composed of fragrant substances. 12---Garlands of flowers. 13---Buttemah or grain soaked and parched. 14---Jowarri. 15---Five lights. 16---Sweetmeats. 17---Betel leaves. 18---Cocoa nut. 19---A sum of money (according to means). 20---Flowers offered by the suppliant, the palms of the hands being joined.

"All these articles, my informant assured me, were offered to the snake in regular succession, one after the other, the worshipper repeating the while certain mantras or incantations. Having offered all these gifts, the worshipper prostrates himself before the snake, and, begging for pardon if he has ever offended against him, craves the snake will continue his favour upon him and protect him from every danger."

In the Oriental Memoirs by Forbes, we are told of the gardeners of Guzerat who would never allow the snakes to be disturbed, calling them "father," "brother," and other familiar and endearing names. The head gardener paid them religious honours. As Deane says, "here we observe a mixture of the original Serpent Worship, with the more modern doctrine of transmigration."

Still more striking is the information in Purchas's Pilgrims, that a king of Calicut built cottages for live serpents, whom he tended with peculiar care, and made it a capital crime for any person in his dominions to destroy a snake. "The natives," he says, "looked upon serpents as endued with divine spirits."

Then there is the festival called "The Feast of the Serpents," at which every worshipper, in the hope of propitiating the reptiles during the ensuing year, sets by a portion of his rice for the hooded snake on the outside of his house.

The deities of India and the wonderful temples and caves, as those at Salsette and Elephanta, as may be seen in Maurice's Indian Antiquities, Moor's Hindu Pantheon, The Asiatic Researches, Faber's Pagan Idolatry and numerous other works, are universally adorned with, or represented by this great symbol. Thus we have the statue of Jeyne, the Indian Æsculapius, turbaned by a seven-headed snake; that of Vishnu on a rock in the Ganges, reposing on a coiled serpent whose numerous folds form a canopy over the sleeping god; Parus Nauth symbolized by a serpent; Jagan-Nath worshipped under the form of a seven-headed dragon.

Hari appears to be one of the titles of Vishnu---that of the deity in his preserving quality---and his appearance on the rock, as just mentioned, is thus noticed in Wilkin's Hitopadesa: "Nearly opposite Sultan Ganj, a considerable town in the province of Bahar, there stands a rock of granite, forming a small island in the Ganges, known to Europeans by the name of 'the rock of Ichangiri,' which is highly worthy of the traveller's notice for the vast number of images carved upon every part of its surface. Among the rest there is Hari, of a gigantic size, recumbent upon a coiled serpent, whose heads (which are numerous) the artist has contrived to spread into a kind of canopy over the sleeping god; and from each of its mouths issues a forked tongue, seeming to threaten instant death to any whom rashness might prompt to disturb him. The whole lies almost clear of the block on which it is hewn. It is finely imagined and is executed with great skill. The Hindus are taught to believe that at the end of every Calpa (creation or formation) all things are absorbed in the Deity, and that in the interval of another creation, he reposeth himself upon the serpent Sesha (duration) who is also called Ananta (endlessness)."

Moor says Garuda was an animal---half bird, half man---and was the vahan or vehicle of Vishnu, also Arun's younger brother. He is sometimes described in the manner that our poets and painters describe a griffin or a cherub; and he is placed at the entrance of the passes leading to the Hindu garden of Eden, and there appears in the character of a destroying angel in as far as he resists the approach of serpents, which in most systems of poetical mythology appears to have been the beautiful, deceiving, insinuating form that sin originally assumed. Garuda espoused a beautiful woman; the tribes of serpents, alarmed thereat, lest his progeny should, inheriting his propensities, overpower them, waged fierce war against him; but he destroyed them all, save one, which he placed as an ornament about his neck. In the Elephanta cave Garuda is often seen with this appendage; and some very old gold coins are in existence depicting him with snakes or elephants in his talons and beaks. Destroyer of serpents, Naganteka, is one of his names.

He was of great use to Krishna in clearing the country round Dwarka (otherwise Dravira) from savage ferocious animals and noxious reptiles. Vishnu had granted to Garuda the power of destroying his as well as Siva's enemies; also generally those guilty of constant uncleanness, unbelievers, dealers in iniquity, ungrateful persons, those who slander their spiritual guides, or defiled their beds; but forbade him to touch a Brahman, whatever was his guilt, as the pain of disobedience would be a scorching pain in his throat, and any attack on a holy or pious person would be followed by a great diminution of strength. By mistake, however, Garuda sometimes seized a priest or a religious man, but was admonished and punished in the first case by the scorching flame, and was unable, even when he had bound him in his den, to hurt the man of piety. "To Rama also, in the war of Lauka, Garuda was eminently useful: in Rama's last conflict with Ravana

---

[11] Asiatic Res., vol. 5, p. 514.

the latter was not overcome without the aid of Garuda, sent by Vishnu to destroy the serpent-arrows of Ravana. These arrows are called "Sharpa-vana" (in the current dialect Sarpa a snake), is corrupted into Saap or S~mp and vana, an arrow, into ban) and had the faculty of separating, between the bow and the object, into many parts, each becoming a serpent. Viswamitra conferred upon Rama the power of transforming his arrows into "Garuda-vanas," they similarly separating themselves into "Garuda's," the terror and destroyer of the Sarpa.

Some legends make Garuda the offspring of Kasyapa and Diti. This all-prolific dame laid an egg, which, it was predicted, would preserve her deliverer from some great affliction. After a lapse of five hundred years Garuda sprang from the egg, flew to the abode of Indra, extinguished the fire that surrounded it, conquered its guards, the devatas, and bore off the amrita (ambrosia) which enabled him to liberate his captive mother. A few drops of this immortal beverage falling on the species of grass called "Kusa," it became eternally consecrated; and the serpents greedily licking it up so lacerated their tongues with the sharp grass that they have ever since remained forked; but the boon of eternity was ensured to them by their thus partaking of the immortal fluid. This cause of snakes having forked tongues is still, in the tales of India, popularly attributed to the above greediness; and thier supposed immortality may have originated in some such stories as these; a small portion of amrita, as in the case of Rahu, would ensure them this boon.

In all mythological language the snake is an emblem of immortality: its endless figure when its tail is inserted in its mouth, and the annual renewal of its skin and vigour, afford symbols of continued youth and eternity; and its supposed medicinal or life-preserving qualities may also have contributed to the fabled honours of the serpent tribe. In Hindu mythology serpents are of universal occurrence and importance; in some shape or other they abound in all directions; a similar state of things prevails in Greece and Egypt. Ingenious and learned authors attribute this universality of serpent form to the early and all pervading prevalence of sin, which, in this identical shape, they tell us, and as indeed we all know, is as old as the days of our greatest grandmother: thus much as to its age, when there was but one woman; its prevalence, now there are so many, this is no place to discuss.

If such writers were to trace the allegories of Sin and Death, and the end of their empire, they might discover further allusions to the Christian dispensation in the traditions of the Hindus than have hitherto been published---Krishna crushing, but not destroying the type of Siva, has often been largely discussed. Garuda is also the proverbial, but not the utter destroyer of serpents, for he spared one, they and their archetype being, in reference to created beings, eternal. His continual and destined state of warfare with serpents, a shape mostly assumed by the enemies of the virtuous incarnations or deified heroes of the Hindus, is a continued allegory of the conflicts between Vice and Virtue so infinitely personified. Garuda, at length, appears the coadjutor of all virtuous sin-subduing efforts, as the vehicle of the chastening and triumphant party, and conveys him on the wings of the winds to the regions of eternal day.

CHAPTER XI

Upwards of sixty years ago, there was opened at the Egyptian Hall, Piccadilly, what was described as the "Unique Exhibition called Ancient Mexico; collected on the spot in 1823, by the assistance of the Mexican Government, by W. Bullock, F. L. S. , &c., &c." The illustration attached to a published description of this collection shows that it contained reproductions of some of the most remarkable of the serpent deities to be found in the temples of the western parts of America, and the following extract will prove interesting to our readers.

"The rattlesnake appears to have been the most general object of worship, veneration, and fear; indeed it occurs in some manner combined with almost every other, and is still found in many of the Indian villages. It remains in Tezcuco, quite perfect at the present time. Broken fragments may be met with in the exterior of the houses in Mexico in several places; the great head placed at the left of the sacrificial stone is cast from one in the corner of the fine building used for the Government Lottery Office, and exposed to the street. It must have belonged to an idol at least seventy feet long, probably in the great temple, and broken and buried at the Conquest. They are generally in a coiled up state, with the tail or rattle on the back, but they vary in their size and position. The finest that is known to exist, I discovered in the destered part of the Cloister of the Dominican Convent opposite the Palace of the Inquisition. It is coiled up in an irritated erect position, with the jaws extended, and in the act of gorging an elegantly dressed female, who appears in the mouth of the enormous reptile, crushed and lacerated, a disgusting detail withal too horrible for description.

"Turning to a letter from Cortes to Charles V., as given by Humboldt, we read, 'From the square we proceeded to the great temle, but before we entered it we made a circuit through a number of large courts, the smallest of which appeared to me to contain more ground than the great square in Salamanca, with double enclosures built of lime and stone, and the courts paved with large white cut stone, very clean; or, where not paved, they were plastered and polished. When we approached the gate of the great temple, to which the ascent was by a hundred and fourteen steps, and before we had mounted one of them, Montezuma sent down to us six priests and two of his noblemen to carry Cortes up, as they had done their sovereign, which he politely declined. When we had ascended to the summit of the temple, we observed on the platform as we passed the large stone whereon were placed the victims who were to be sacrificed. Here was a great figure which resembled a dragon, and much blood fresh spilt. Cortes then addressing himself to Montezuma requested that he would do him the favour to show us his gods. Montezuma, having first consulted his priests, led us into a tower where there was a kind of saloon. here were two altars highly adorned, with richly wrought timbers on the roof, and over the altars gigantic figures resembling very fat men. The one on the right was Huitzilopochtli their war god, with a great face and terrible eyes, this figure was entirely covered with gold and jewels, and his body bound with golden serpents, in his right hand he held a bow, and in his left a bundle of arrows. The little idol which stood by him represented his page, and bore a lance and target richly ornamented with gold and jewels. The great idol had round his neck the figures of human heads and hearts made of pure gold and silver, ornamented with precious stones of a blue colour. Before the idol was a pan of incense, with three hearts of human victims which were there burning, mixed with copal. The whole of that apartment, both walls and floor, was stained with human blood in such quantity as to give a very offensive smell. On the left was the other great figure, with a countenance like a bear, and great shining eyes of the polished substance whereof their mirrors are made. The body of this idol was also covered with jewels. These two deities it was said were brothers; the name of the last was Tezcatepuca, and he was the god of the infernal regions. He presided, according to their notions, over the souls of men. His body was covered with figures representing little devils with tails of serpents, and the walls and pavement of this temple were so besmeared with blood that they gave off a worse odour than all the slaughter-houses of Castille. An offering lay before him of five human hearts. In the summit of the temple, and in a recess the timber of which was highly ornamented, we saw a figure half human and the other half resembling an alligator, inlaid with jewels, and partly covered with a mantle. This idol was said to contain the germ and origin of all created things, and was the god of harvests and fruits. The walls and altars were bestained like the rest, and so offensive that we thought we never could get out soon enough.

"In this place they had a drum of most enormous size, the head of which was made of the skins of large serpents. This instrument when struck resounded with a noise that could be heard to the distance of two leagues, and so doleful that it deserved to be named the music of the infernal regions; and with their horrible sounding horns and trumpets, their great knives for sacrifice, their human victims, and their blood besprinkled altars, I devoted them and all their wickedness to God's vengeance, and thought that the time would never arrive that I should escape from this scene of butchery, horrible smells, and more detestable sights.

" 'On the site of the church, called St. Jago el Taltelulco, was a temple, which, we have already observed, was surrounded with courts as large as the square of Salamanca. At a little distance from it stood a tower, a true hell or habitation for demons, with a mouth, resembling that of an enormous monster, wide open, and ready as it were to devour those who entered. At the door stood frightful idols; by it was a place for sacrifice, and within, boilers and pots full of water to dress the flesh of the victims which were eaten by the priests. The idols were like serpents and devils, and before them were tables and knives for sacrifice, the place being covered with the blood which was spilt on those occasions. The furniture was like that of a butcher" stall, and I never gave this accursed building any name except that of hell. Having passed this, we saw great piles of wood, and a reservoir of water supplied by a pipe from the great aqueduct; and crossing a court we came to another temple, wherein were the tombs of the Mexican nobility, it was begrimed with soot and blood. Next to this was another, full of skeletons and piles of bones, each kept apart, but regularly arranged. In each temple were idols, and each had also its particular priests, who wore long vestments of black, their long hair was clotted together, and their ears lacerated in honour of their gods.'"

Mr. Bullock then proceeds to describe a cast of the great idol of the goddess of war, which he had brought to England with him.

"This monstrous idol, before which thousands of human victims were annually sacrificed on the altar is, with its pedestal, about twelve feet high and four feet wide, it is sculptured out of one solid piece of grey basalt. Its form is partly human, and the rest composed of rattlesnakes and the tiger. The head, enormously wide, seems that of two rattlesnakes united, the fangs hanging out of the mouth, on which the still palpitating hearts of the unfortunate victims were rubbed as an act of the most acceptable oblation. The body is that of a deformed human frame, and the place of arms supplied by the heads of rattlesnakes placed on square plinths and united by fringed ornaments. Round the waist is a girdle, which was originally covered with gold, and beneath this, reaching nearly to the ground and partly covering its deformed cloven feet, a drapery entirely composed of wreathed rattlesnakes which the nations call cohuatlicuye or garments of serpents, on each side of which is a winged termination of the feathers of the vulture. Between the feet, descending from the body, another wreathed serpent rested its head on the ground, and the whole composition of this deity is strictly appropriate to the infernal purpose for which it was used, and with which the personal ornaments too well accord. From the neck, spreading over its deformed breast, is a necklace composed of human hands, hearts, and skulls---fit emblems of the sanguinary rites daily performed in its honour.

"The death's head and mutilated hands, four of which surround the bosom of the goddess, remind us of the terrible sacrifices of Teoquawhquat, celebrated in the fifteenth century period of thirteen days after the summer solstice, in honour of the god of war and his female companion, Teoyamiqui. The mutilated hands alternate with the figure of certain vases in which incense was burnt. These vases were called Topxicalli, bags in the form of calabashes. This idol was sculptured on every side, even beneath where was represented Mictlanteuchtli, the Lord of the place of the dead; it cannot be doubted, but that it was supported in the air by means of two columns, on which rested the arms. According to this whimsical arrangement, the head of the idol was probably elevated five or six metres above the pavement of the temple, so that the priests dragging their unfortunate victims to the altar made them pass under the figure of Mictlanteuchtli. The Viceroy of Mexico transported this monument to the University which he thought the most proper place to preserve one of the most curious remains of American antiquity. The Professors of the University, monks of the Order of St. Dominic, were unwilling to expose this idol to the sight of the Mexican youth, and caused it to be reburied in one of the passages of the College. But Mr. Humboldt had it disinterred at the request of the Bishop of Monterey.

"A highly curious specimen of Mexican sculpture is an exceeding hard stone resembling hornstein, a course kind of jade, it is a species of compact talc, of most elaborate workmanship, and the bust of a priest, or perhaps of the idol representing the Sun. The head is crowned with a high mitre-shaped cap, decorated with jewels and feathers, it has long pendant earrings. The hands are raised, the right sustains something resembling a knotted club, while the left takes hold of a festoon of flowers which descends from the head; all the other parts are covered with the scales and rattles of the deadly reptile."

Our prescribed limits are now reached, and we are able to add but little to what has already been advanced exhibiting the widespread prevalence of this singular form of worship. Again and again has wonderment been expressed that it should ever be possible for a creature so disgusting to become an object of worship, but so it has been, and no age or country seems to have been strange to it. Very early indeed in history men began to worship a serpent, that brazen one of the Exodus, which Hezekiah destroyed on account of the idolatry into which it led the people. But if that object was put away, the hope that the worship would cease was vain, for it started up amongst the Assyrians, the Chaldeans, the Phœnicians, the Egyptians, and spread into Greece, Esthonia, Finland, Italy, Persia, Hindustan, Ceylon, China, Japan, Burmah, Java, Arabia, Syria, Ethiopia, Britain, Mexico, and Peru.

Such was its extent---wide as the world itself, and vast beyond estimate or description was its influence over the minds of those who came within its reach. Let the curious reader who would know more, and who would make himself acquainted with the multitudinous forms in which the emblem was depicted, study the works of such writers as Kingsford and Montfaucon, with their numerous and well executed plates, and he will meditate with astonishment upon the singular fascination which this repulsive reptile seems to have exercised over the human mind. He is said, we know, so to fascinate the victim he is about to seize as his prey that the unhappy creature is deprived of all power of resistance, a fascination no less overwhelming seems to have paralyzed the human mind and caused it to adopt from some cause or other such a repelling reptile as an object of worship. The spell is broken now, however, and but little remains of what was once so universal, beyond the earth mounds where its temples stood and the half ruined sculptures collected in the museums of civilized countries.

www.ingramcontent.com/pod-product-compliance
Lightning Source LLC
Chambersburg PA
CBHW071730090426
42738CB00011B/2443